THE GARDEN
AT FOREST HALL

The Garden at Forest Hall

PHOTOGRAPHY BY SIMON GRIFFITHS

Susan Irvine

VIKING

Pages i, ii–iii The front garden at Forest Hall.

Page v Quinces on the walnut platter that Paul Nordanus made (see page 124).

Opposite Thousands of muscari are among the heralds of spring.

Page viii Dry-stone walls are a feature of the garden.

Pages x–xi The front garden in spring.

Endpapers Front: 'Dunwich Rose' hips (left) and cardoon seed heads (right).

Back: map of the garden, by Tim Barbour.

Viking
Penguin Books Australia Ltd
250 Camberwell Road
Camberwell, Victoria 3124, Australia
Penguin Books Ltd
Harmondsworth, Middlesex, England
Penguin Putnam Inc.
375 Hudson Street, New York, New York 10014, USA
Penguin Books Canada Limited
10 Alcorn Avenue, Toronto, Ontario, Canada M4V 3B2
Penguin Books (NZ) Ltd
Cnr Rosedale and Airborne Roads, Albany, Auckland, New Zealand
Penguin Books (South Africa) (Pty) Ltd
24 Sturdee Avenue, Rosebank, Johannesburg 2196, South Africa
Penguin Books India (P) Ltd
11, Community Centre, Panchsheel Park, New Delhi 110 017, India

First published by Penguin Books Australia Ltd 2002

10 9 8 7 6 5 4 3 2 1

Text copyright © Susan Irvine 2002
Photographs copyright © Simon Griffiths 2002

Designed by Tony Palmer, Penguin Design Studio
Photography by Simon Griffiths, except for: 'Abraham Darby' (page 65), supplied with permission by
Dorling Kindersley Limited, London; and photographs on pages 46 and 138, supplied by Susan Irvine
Typeset in 10.5 pt Fairfield by Post Typesetters, Brisbane, Queensland
Scanning and separations by Splitting Image P/L, Blackburn, Victoria
Printed and bound in Singapore by Imago Productions

National Library of Australia
Cataloguing-in-Publication data:

Irvine, Susan, 1928– .
    The garden at Forest Hall

    Includes index.
    ISBN 0 670 89657 8.

    1. Irvine, Susan, 1928– – Homes and haunts – Tasmania.
    2. Gardens – Tasmania. I. Griffiths, Simon (Simon John). II. Title.

635.09946

www.penguin.com.au

For William and Sarah Bonnily,
who built Forest Hall, planted its trees
and established the first garden.

Contents

History repeats itself

WE HAD BEEN spending a holiday in northern Tasmania, as we had done every year since we were married – fishing holidays they were. We had bought, a few years earlier, a little A-frame house in picturesque Golden Valley just below towering Quamby Bluff, twenty minutes' drive from Deloraine and 50 kilometres west of Launceston on the road to the Great Lake. This wonderful stretch of water is a mecca for fly-fishermen from all round the world. While Bill fished I pottered about in the embryo garden, looked at historic houses, visited other people's gardens and the tempting specialist nurseries Tasmania is renowned for. But our remote cottage was never regarded in the light of a possible permanent home. There was no thought of our ever spending more than a week or so there a couple of times a year.

On a clear, sunny day in December 1995 – a typical Tasmanian summer day, warm and still, the sky an untroubled blue and the mountains two shades darker – I was driving along the Bass Highway with a friend. Michael was a non-fishing friend, so while Bill fished I had been detailed to entertain him. This was not difficult. He was a delightful companion, a frequenter of art galleries, antique shops and heritage buildings, and had

---

Opposite Forest Hall was sad and neglected when we first saw it, but nothing could mar the beauty of the grand front door, with its Gothic panes and sidelights.

In the wide and spacious entrance hall of the abandoned house we found a cedar staircase curving up to the first storey. Eventually, with house restorations complete, our table piano, built in London in 1790, was to be at home in this setting.

spent several years on the council of the National Gallery in Canberra.

Just past Elizabeth Town – two churches, one pub, one service station and nothing else – we saw on our left, across a garden full of ancient trees, a fine old Georgian house, and all along its dilapidated fence were estate agents' signs. It was for sale.

'Stop! Stop!' cried Michael. 'Look at that! We'll have to go in.'

My mind went back to Bleak House – back nearly twenty years. In just this way had I found it. A little old bluestone cottage unloved and uncared for, standing by the side of the Calder Highway in Victoria. I had bought it on impulse. Fallen in love at first sight. Now history was about to repeat itself. But this stone house, unlike Bleak House, was stately and imposing, although obviously suffering from neglect. It stood on a slight rise looking down over its own parkland and across to the lofty blue ranges beyond.

I did a U-turn and drove into the gateway. The rusted farm gate was half open and along the drive were several handwritten notices advising the curious that this was private property and trespasers [sic] were liable to be prosecuted. Nothing daunted, we drove slowly towards the house. The drive was rough and overhung by giant trees that cast a deep shade. I mentally rehearsed the speech I would make to the irate owners when they appeared. About a hundred metres from the gate the drive swung abruptly to the right and we found ourselves at the entrance to a sunny courtyard behind the house.

'This,' said Michael, 'would have to be one of the most beautiful houses I have seen.'

He was out of the car before I had properly come to a standstill, exclaiming about the perfect proportions, the northerly aspect of this courtyard, the remnants of a garden. No owners appeared. No fierce proprietorial dogs. Nothing. This splendid old house was quite deserted. Michael decreed that we were to drive forthwith into nearby Deloraine and knock up one of the agents whose boards were defacing the fence. We chose one at random and started off. I ventured to ask on the way which of us was ostensibly showing an interest in purchasing the property.

Opposite The Georgian house at Forest Hall stood on a slight rise looking down over parkland.

'Well, you of course,' he said.

But bitter disappointment awaited us in Deloraine. The agent, slightly amused by our transparent excitement, announced that he had in fact sold the house the day before. He smiled at my patent disbelief and reiterated that it was sold – sold moreover to two buyers. The house, it transpired, stood on 300 acres (I never can think in hectares): one buyer wanted the house and 10 acres surrounding it; the other was interested in the rest, presently operating in part as a raspberry farm.

Rather exasperated but scenting the possibility of some future sale if these main-landers were crazy enough, he agreed reluctantly to show us through the house – Forest Hall it was called – but emphasised that we should abandon any hope of purchasing it.

We collected Bill – a rather reluctant Bill, who had had a less than satisfactory day with the trout – and drove back to Forest Hall, up the drive and into the sun-filled courtyard at the back. Here the agent left us while he went round the house to let us in. The moment he opened the back door I was gone. The hall was wide and spacious, the width of a room, and facing us at the far end was one of the loveliest front entrances I have seen: double doors of polished cedar, which spanned the whole width of the hall, an arched fanlight with gothic panes at each end and sidelights. Richly polished floorboards, and an exquisite staircase curv-ing up to the top floor. This was, quite simply, the house of one's dreams.

But we didn't need a house. We had one in Victoria, with a lovely garden into the bar-gain – a garden that represented nine years of hard labour. We didn't live in Tasmania and had no thought of doing so. And moreover, as the agent continued to emphasise, this house was sold.

There were four rooms downstairs, each with an open fireplace and a cedar mantel-piece untouched by paint. The two front rooms opened into the garden through elegant french doors: tall, six-paned french doors, also in polished cedar, with panelled surrounds. The two back rooms, which we had seen from the courtyard, were flooded in sunshine.

I literally ran up the stairs to see what was above. Two huge front bedrooms looked out across the trees to the purple-blue of the Western Tiers. Off one of them was a tiny room, papered with faded rosebuds, that opened through french doors onto nothing but the veranda roof. A nursery perhaps. At the back were two more big bedrooms. No bathroom. From a door in the upstairs hall a staircase led up to the roof. The new owners, the agent said, planned to make four more rooms up there and run Forest Hall as a bed and breakfast place. I shuddered.

The kitchen, set at right angles to the main building, was appalling the agent informed us. We wouldn't want to see it. There was no hot water, no sink, not even a stove and it was indescribably dirty. It would need to be entirely rebuilt. He steered us towards the back door. But I didn't want to miss any of it. Reluctantly he opened the kitchen door and stood aside to let us in. He was quite right. It was unusable. Not only was there no sink, no stove, no hot water, but someone had cut off a section of it to create a (very grubby, very makeshift) fibro pantry. And there were holes in the floor – big ones you could fall down. However, the stone walls, unlike those in the main rooms, which were plastered, were rough and unlined. The four big windows were multi-paned and deep silled. The ceiling was spanned at 60-centimetre intervals by heavy black beams, festooned with cobwebs. The bread oven with its solid black iron door was still intact. And the door into the courtyard, when it creaked open, let in the sunshine and a view of a spreading chestnut on the far side of the drive.

'You see,' began the agent, then stopped as he caught sight of my face. Mainlanders were strange cattle.

Historic houses are not among Bill's interests. He had wandered about, hands in pockets, saying little and apparently noticing less. But now he turned to me, his puzzlement verging on incredulity, and said 'You really love this, don't you?'

'I'd kill for it,' I replied.

From then on he took an interest. He turned to the agent.

'You say you have two buyers – have you got the subdivision through and are the two sales tied together? And have both the purchasers their finance up front?'

'Well, no, not yet . . .'

'When the sale falls through get in touch with me,' Bill said and turned to leave.

We didn't look at the 300 acres. We didn't inspect the stables or the barn or the blacksmith's cottage. We didn't even walk round the overgrown garden. After all, the property was sold.

Committed

THREE MONTHS PASSED and gradually I thought less about Forest Hall, stopped making plans for it. By this time it was probably in the process of being converted to a B & B, the gracious rooms split up to make provision for ensuites with spa baths, the stately entrance hall turned into an office with receptionist's desk and racks of tourist brochures.

We were on holiday in New Zealand, staying at a hotel in Wellington, when the phone rang in our room. It was the agent from Deloraine. He had shown remarkable tenacity and ingenuity in tracking us down to announce, somewhat apologetically, that if we were still interested that place we'd looked at with him was back on the market. The sales had fallen through. But most likely, he surmised, we had found something else by now.

It was only then, I think, when it seemed that it might be still within our grasp, that I fully realised how many dreams I had woven round it, what a prominent place it had come to occupy in my thoughts for the future.

Bill was due to retire in something under a year. If a radical change was to be made in our lifestyle this might be the time to make it. We were not keen to stay in Gisborne indefinitely. The little town that had resembled an English village when we moved there

---

Opposite An ancient walnut tree was evidence of the existence
in earlier days of a productive orchard.

had grown steadily and now new subdivisions came right to our back fence. And the garden at Erinvale, built on the side of a very steep hill, would become increasingly difficult to manage. But our plans for the future had certainly never included a farm – in Tasmania or anywhere else.

'No,' I said to the agent patiently waiting on the other end of the phone. 'No. We haven't really looked at anything else. And yes, yes,' with more conviction, 'of course we are still interested.' And then and there I asked him to hold it for us and undertook to go down to Tasmania as soon as we returned home.

Bill was, predictably, not convinced. He loved Tasmania, and fly-fishing, for which it is famous, is the joy of his life. Without doubt he would want in his retirement to spend a considerable time each year up at the Great Lake in pursuit of trout. But this was some-thing else.

'What on earth are we to do with 300 acres?' he asked.

'Sell them,' I answered promptly.

The agent in our brief telephone conversation had told me that the subdivision had been approved. It was lack of funds that had caused the sales to fall through. So we would be able to keep the house on 10 acres and dispose of the rest.

As soon as we returned from New Zealand we booked a flight to Tasmania so that we could have a proper look at this virtually unknown quantity I had more or less undertaken to buy. We arrived on a cool autumn morning and went straight out to Forest Hall. The house was every bit as imposing as I remembered it. We decided to park the car at the gate and walk up the drive. The aged oaks and aspens that lined it on the right side were just turning gold and their leaves made a thick carpet on the ground.

The first shock awaited us just inside the gate, on the edge of the drive. Surveyors' pegs are unmistakable. This peg excluded the tall hawthorn hedge on our left, which ran from the gate up past the house. It excluded the paddock beyond the hedge, with five venerable oak trees, chestnuts, an elm, a larch, a splendid blackwood – and inevitably and unfortunately a mountain of blackberry and, the curse of farmers in Tasmania, a rampant growth of ragwort.

Worse was in store. The line for the subdivision swung round the edge of the drive, barely 50 metres from the back door, and excluded the blacksmith's cottage and the stables beyond. It was not to be contemplated. Not only would we lose these fine buildings, an essential part of the history of Forest Hall, we would also lose all privacy and have no control over our environment. We would have trucks, tractors, farm workers and raspberry pickers going up and down at all hours of the day. The whole ambience of the lovely house, the air of history that pervaded it, would be destroyed.

We looked at each other in dismay. Certainly we did not want extensive farming land and all the responsibility that would involve, but this alternative was not to be thought of. There was nothing for it. We would have to buy it as it stood, with 300 acres of as yet unexplored land. Perhaps one of the local farmers would be interested in leasing it. We decided to postpone making a final decision for the time being and go on a tour of the property.

There had once been a garden. There was no doubt of that. The trees alone bore witness to it. As was the case with many of the early colonial homes, whoever had laid out this garden had been strongly influenced by the parklike naturalism of the English landscape tradition. The garden was dominated by the trees – more oaks, elms, lindens, the giant aspens on the drive, two magnificent cedars in front of the house, placed strategically on either side but well back from the front entrance, a towering sequoiadendron, a cluster of robinias, huge hollies and, the greatest thrill of all, another splendid larch. Locals told us later that it is reputedly the best, if not the oldest, larch in northern Tasmania.

There were two groups of the cordylines that seem to have been almost obligatory in early Australian gardens. They sat uneasily among the European trees. The front garden was extensive and there had once been a semicircular drive. At one end of the front veranda was a fine stone horse trough, standing ready to water the horses after what must have been at that time a trying journey from Deloraine to Forest Hall.

To the south-east of the house, facing the road, was the shrubbery. At least, it was obvious that it had once been a shrubbery. It was now a tangled mass of overgrown trees and shrubs all intertwined with blackberry and carpeted with vinca and ivy. There were also the remains of vicious barbed-wire fences, which were discouraging to say the least. We skirted round the shrubbery and postponed any attempt to identify things.

Behind the house to the east, where it was sheltered and sunny, there had clearly

From the top of the hill behind the house Bill and I looked, on our first exploration, across lush farmland to the deep blue of the majestic Western Tiers. *Opposite above* The gnarled, misshapen mulberry we found near the barn was to bear a huge crop of luscious purple berries in the late summer of our first year at Forest Hall. *Opposite below* An aged sequoia, its trunk almost hollow, grew well beyond the confines of the garden.

been a kitchen garden and perhaps an orchard. Here we found peach and nectarine trees, long neglected and unpruned, walnuts and a gnarled old mulberry with an Arthur Rackham face. The beds were a mass of raspberries run wild, potatoes and clumps of outsized rhubarb.

A skilfully constructed dry-stone wall – probably 150 years old and convict built, as was the house – marked the end of the garden. Behind it the ground rose quite steeply so that the stables were two storeys on the side facing towards the house and one on the far side. Further up the hill we found what had once been stockyards, a race and a shearing shed. Much further up again were a perfectly hideous dairy and a coolroom of more recent date. Perhaps they could be demolished, I thought. It wasn't until considerably later that I realised that we were dependent on the run-off from their roofs for our house water, which was pumped down from two big holding tanks.

We were puzzled by the fact that there were oaks, hollies and an elm out in what were now paddocks. Surely the garden had never extended as far as this? And way up beyond the stockyards was a magnificent sequoia. We pushed our way through long grass and a tangle of blackberries and thistles and found, when we reached it, that it was almost entirely hollow. Once there had been a fence round it, presumably to protect it from stock or wildlife.

We returned to the stockyards and discovered on closer examination that what had most recently been a shearing shed had once been a cottage. There was a hearth and the remains of an open fireplace. The windows had had wooden shutters in place of glass, and the whole had been papered. We could just make out a pattern of leaves and ferns on what might have been a gold background. A shepherd's hut? A workman's cottage? Would either of these have had wallpaper? Or had it been the very first house on the property?

Ascending again, we found near the dairy a fine plantation of *Cupressus macrocarpa*, which Bill, who has a fine disregard for botanical nomenclature, promptly christened the Magna Cartas. They were planted so close together that they formed a wall, their trunks joining to make an impenetrable barrier.

The track curved past them and continued to the very top of the hill. We turned to look back at the house and caught our breath at the sheer splendour of what lay below us –

rich red soil and emerald-green fields resembling the proverbial patchwork quilt, the squares divided by hawthorn hedges; lakes reflecting a scud of fluffy white clouds; and the wonderful deep blue of the Western Tiers, dominated to the south-east by Quamby Bluff and to the south-west by rugged, towering Mt Roland. This country knows nothing of the fearful droughts that plague the Tasmanian south and midlands. It is a land of milk and honey and remains lush and green the whole year round.

Our own country – I was now totally committed and considered it such – was divided into separate paddocks by lines of poplars, cypresses and eucalypts obviously planted as windbreaks. We followed one of these lines down into the valley to a huge shallow dam that was home to a family of graceful black swans and a flock of wild ducks. From here we could still see the mountains but no sign of roads or habitation. It was total seclusion.

We pressed on, found three more dams, all comfortingly full, more picturesque windbreaks and stands of tall, white-trunked gums. We came upon a plantation of about a hundred nashi trees, various randomly planted (or even self-seeded?) apples and plums, and acres and acres of raspberries. The canes were totally neglected – wild and overgrown and weed infested. It was several years, I estimated, since they had been cultivated or pruned, but the fruit had clearly been harvested.

We pushed on, through a field of lush lucerne and into a patch of native bush. About half the property, we guessed, was still bush, a safe haven for a multitude of wallabies, poteroos and padimelons, Tasmanian devils, wombats and possums, and flocks of beautiful birds. Bill reminded me that we would be in competition with all of these if and when we came to make a garden. I was reminded of my dear friend and passionate gardener Maria Fawcett and her attitude to the possums that treated her garden as their own demesne. 'There is enough for us all,' she used to say.

As we turned to come back to the house, the sun was going down and the mountains had turned a deep navy blue. Rabbits scuttled out from under our very feet and a stout echidna ambled in leisurely fashion across the track.

The house nestled at the foot of the hill, enfolded by its trees. Despite obvious signs of neglect it looked dignified and gracious. It had about it what is described in many current gardening books as a 'sense of place'. A little tender care would restore it to its former glory.

Bill, who is nothing if not a realist, remarked that a good deal more than a little would be required. It might prove to be a life sentence. But what a project for two people about to retire and not accustomed to idleness. Having seen it and contemplated all the possibilities, a unit in South Yarra, however imposing and even if equipped with every modern convenience the twenty-first century has to offer, seemed unthinkable.

We drove into Deloraine early the next morning and signed the necessary papers.

<hr/>

Opposite It was autumn when we returned to look at Forest Hall and the century-old oaks and aspens along the drive were turning gold.

William Bonnily's legacy

We began our 'tenure of stewardship' in February 1997 – at least I did. Bill was still working in Melbourne so until the following September he commuted, flying up on Monday morning and returning to Forest Hall on Thursday evening.

Immediately the house was overrun by builders. There was a great deal to be done – bathrooms to be created and the kitchen to be totally renovated, the antiquated wiring to be replaced. The installation of efficient heating was a top priority. The lath and plaster ceilings upstairs had to be replaced, and the glass in most of the windows.

Through all the upheaval the old house stood firm. It was at this time that I came across a book by Norman Thelwell, *A Millstone Round My Neck*. I suspect Bill thought it was particularly appropriate to our situation. I was impressed by one passage that could have been written for us: 'It drew me like a magnet and yet at point of contact it held aloof waiting for a sign or password which I did not know. I owned it but it would not be possessed. It held on always to some echo of the past, of the people who built it and worked it through the years.'

Maureen, the vivacious warm-hearted infinitely good-humoured red-haired blue-eyed Irish girl who came one day a week to help me in the house, was convinced the place was haunted. She hated to be left alone here.

I sought information about 'the people who built it and worked it through the years'. It came from a variety of sources.

My first visit was from Molly Pedley, aged ninety-nine. Her son called and asked if he could bring his mother as she had been born here in one of the upstairs rooms. I looked forward to meeting her but wondered how someone of such advanced years would manage the stairs.

I need not have worried. The following Saturday a smart little red car pulled up on the drive and out hopped Molly Pedley, snow-white hair, eyes the blue of a summer sky and a bright blue coat to match. She needed no stick. She positively flew up the stairs and found the room she was looking for.

Back downstairs in the kitchen she reminisced about life at Forest Hall a hundred years ago. Above the kitchen are four tiny interconnected rooms. When we came they had no windows and no lining and there was no staircase. Access had been through a door above the courtyard. These had been the convict quarters, and a ladder had been put up at night and withdrawn when the girls were safely within. By the time Molly lived here convicts were a thing of the past, but she remembered that there had always been maids and these cold and cheerless little rooms had been their quarters. In really cold weather when there was snow or very heavy rain, they would let themselves down into the kitchen through a trapdoor in the ceiling rather than descend outside.

An extract from a National Trust publication confirmed Molly's claim that Forest Hall had been built in the late 1840s or early 1850s by a William Bonnily and had remained in the Bonnily family until the 1930s. The census of 1848 shows William Bonnily living at Elizabeth Town with six servants, all convicts.

Other people contacted us. Mary MacRae, a great-great-grand-daughter of William Bonnily and Sarah, his wife, wrote to us. From her we learnt that William and Sarah's first child, Elizabeth, had died when she was only 4 years old and it was thought that William had named Elizabeth Town for her.

A visitor from California told of boyhood holidays spent here towards the end of World War II when Forest Hall was almost self-supporting, with extensive orchards and vegetable gardens, two sturdy draught horses in the stable and milking cows to be brought in every morning and evening.

Gradually we were piecing things together. Then came a real scoop. A local historian

brought us a copy of a little book entitled *The Bonnily Family 1803–1996*, put together by one of William's descendants. This too confirmed that it was indeed William Bonnily who had built Forest Hall. He had come from Scotland at the age of 20 as a free settler in 1824. He had worked for a time as a blacksmith in Launceston before acquiring his first grant of land, in the midlands, near Epping Forest. Descendants believe he had learnt and taught various trades in Scotland to equip him for emigrating.

The house on the land where William Bonnily first farmed is still standing, and the road to it is called Forest Hall Road. Bill and I contacted the present owners and spent a fascinating morning there. The house resembles our own in some respects but it was never completed. The staircase goes up into roof space that had clearly been intended for rooms. Most interesting to me was the fact that even here, with such a tremendous task in front of him, a young wife and a tiny daughter, water shortages (which finally drove him out) and the ravages of bushrangers, William Bonnily had found time to plant trees. Many of them still stand – elms and robinias and the inevitable palms.

William moved later to Elizabeth Town and built a house, which he called Rubicon Side (since burnt down). Here too he planted trees. But more and of greater variety than at his first home. For the most part they were the ones that he was to plant later at Forest Hall. They were not just any trees but the lords of the forest.

And they are still standing – the oaks and elms, lindens and

Opposite The kitchen, derelict when we bought Forest Hall, after restoration took on something of the character it must once have had when Sarah Bonnily presided over it.

21

sequoias – although the house has gone, replaced by a modern brick veneer.

Gardens are fragile things, often hardly outliving their original owners. But trees are a different matter. William Bonnily, working to establish his property at Forest Hall a century and a half ago, bequeathed a great legacy to all who should follow him. He was an astute farmer and businessman and engaged in many real estate transactions. He was close to 50 when he built Forest Hall and had become a wealthy man. The only photograph we have shows him as a portly and dignified old fellow with a flowing white beard, a typical nineteenth-century paterfamilias. By the time he came to Forest Hall he was in a position to build a substantial house and lay out an extensive garden.

Since William Bonnily's day Forest Hall has passed through many hands, but the trees he planted have survived and while undoubtedly some things have died the basic lay-out of the garden has probably not changed much. Although of course I have planted many roses – and will plant more – I have no desire to alter too radically the garden we have inherited. And we have planted trees as future replacements for those that might in time succumb to old age, seeking to leave in our turn a legacy for those who will come after us.

William and Sarah Bonnily.

The lake

EARLY IN THE PIECE we tackled the question of water. Elizabeth Town was reputed to have a high rainfall (100 centimetres per annum was mentioned), but I was not prepared to rely on it. I had gardened before with insufficient water – at Gisborne, where water was often rationed towards the end of a long, hot summer – and watched precious plants parched and stressed and even dying for want of a drink. This was something I did not want to go through again.

It was a choice between putting down a bore and constructing a dam. The second alternative seemed to me by far the preferable one. There is nothing attractive about a bore but a stretch of water can add another dimension to the garden. For there is something magical about water – a stream, a lake, a fountain, even quite a modest pond can alter a whole landscape.

The local farmers of course assured us that a dam would be quite unsuitable in this country. It would leak, we were told. But there were in fact four dams already for stock. Farmers are not always logical. They are also notoriously pessimistic. We decided to ignore their dire predictions.

Siting the dam presented few problems. The paddock next to the garden on the south-east side was ruled out. I did not yet know how far the garden might ultimately extend. But beyond this was a paddock enclosed on three sides by high hawthorn hedges, which hid it from the house. In the middle was a low-lying area greener than the rest and with clumps of rushes. A spring perhaps?

Nothing disturbs the tranquillity of the garden as early
morning mist lingers on the lake we put in.

We had not yet been through a winter, which is the time of highest rainfall. We held lengthy discussions with the local dozer driver, who has a great reputation as a builder of dams. He was confident. He stopped just short of a firm guarantee. So we went ahead. He was here for a week and those seven days saw a nondescript paddock transformed into a huge basin that, he assured us, would when full hold over 10 million litres of water.

The first real rain came in April. June saw torrential downpours and before the end of July the water in the dam reached the overflow point. It was a triumph. Since then we have never lacked water and I am able to run sprinklers and trickle lines as often as I please. There are springs up in the hills behind the house and the water in the dam is clean and clear.

I had not intended to extend the cultivated garden to take in the dam paddock. There was, in any case, very little room there. The dam reached almost to the surrounding hawthorn hedges. But on a trip to Melbourne I made the acquaintance of the Yunnan poplar (*Populus yunnanensis*). I was, of all unlikely places to find a tree, in David Jones. I was on the second floor and suddenly became aware of some wonderful foliage beyond the window. I asked the man serving me if he knew what the tree was.

'I'm so glad you asked me,' he said, 'because I only found out yesterday. It's the Yunnan poplar.'

It was late autumn. The tree reached to the second-floor windows and was a sheet of gold. If it could grow in these conditions – in the heart of the city surrounded by fumes and smog, and embedded in asphalt – it could grow anywhere.

As soon as I returned to Tasmania I looked for it and without too much trouble located six. I planted them fairly close together round a huge protruding rock and they have grown with amazing rapidity. This year I think they will rival that one outside David Jones.

The rabbits broke off a couple of low branches, which I put in as cuttings. They took and are doing well. Obviously I could have a forest of Yunnan poplars if I wished. They are reputed to grow to 25 metres. And they do not sucker as many poplars do.

On the side nearest the house, at the highest point of the dam paddock, tucked in under the hawthorn hedge, we discovered an old stone cattle trough. We cut the hedge away from it and made quite a wide opening to link it to the paddocks on both sides. Eventually I would find a way of incorporating it into the garden.

We cleaned the trough, filled it and were delighted to find that it held water. So I sent away to Norgate's well-known perennial nursery in Victoria for fifty *Iris kaempferi*, the water iris, in shades of white, pale blue, deeper blue and purple. I planted them round the cattle trough and in a wide swathe leading down to the dam. Each year I have added more, hoping eventually to reach the water's edge.

A friend with a rambling country garden gave me dozens of *I. sibirica*, white, pale blue and purple, and these were added to the iris bed. From other parts of the garden I dug up clumps of the yellow *I. pseudacorus*, the water flag, and white *I. ochroleuca*, the swamp iris, and planted them in the wetter parts, where the spring water flows in, sometimes for months.

One day just after the iris planting was completed, I was walking along a street in Launceston when I came upon a huge wicker basket sitting on the footpath and filled with scarlet tulips – not the genuine article and not the sort my mother would ever have contemplated buying, but artificial ones. It was winter and there was nothing much in the garden so I succumbed and went in, intending to buy a dozen or so.

Inside, sitting on the counter, was the most wonderful frog, squatting on his hind legs and holding an absurd umbrella over his head. It was Mr Toad himself. I had an instant mental picture of him perched on the edge of the cattle trough or on a flat stone like a lily pad, surrounded by the water irises. I came home with not only twenty artificial scarlet tulips but also a magnificent bronze frog.

It was at this point that Bill decided that the stretch of tranquil water, with its beautiful reflections of cloud and trees, its copse of young poplars, its iris bed and the added air of distinction lent by Mr Toad, should no longer go by the plebeian name of 'the dam'. From henceforth, he decreed, it should be known as 'the lake'.

Mr Toad, holding his absurd
umbrella, stands on the edge of
the stone trough near the lake,
surrounded by *Iris kaempferi*,
the water iris, just coming
into flower.

Daffodils

AMONG THE FIRST THINGS I planted at Forest Hall was a variegated dogwood, *Cornus controversa* 'Variegata'. I love the way the branches grow in tiers and the leaves are edged in white. I bought it in a 20-centimetre pot and decided to plant it at the back of the shrubbery. In digging a hole big enough to accommodate it, I unearthed no fewer than sixty daffodil bulbs. This was the first indication I had that there were bulbs in the garden.

It was towards the end of April that I found the first ones poking through in the paddock that separated the shrubbery from the lake. We had had a good – and much needed – autumn rain, which had set the springs running up in the hills. After three days of steady downpour the sun peeped through the clouds and I walked across to see whether our new dam, now approaching its overflow point, was holding firm. It was. The water was still running in steadily at the far end.

I walked slowly round the entire circumference, making a mental note of the level of the water as measured on the rocky outcrops – a swan's nest that I had seen earlier built rather precariously, I thought, on a rock was now almost submerged.

On my way back to the house I noticed the unmistakable spear of a bulb pushing through the grass. I knelt to examine it and found it to be one of a small colony – a closely knit family of at least ten. Luckily our tenant's cows had recently been grazing in this paddock – we did not yet consider it part of the garden – so the grass had been eaten down, allowing me to see the bulbs. Cows, fortunately, in company with rabbits, don't eat bulbs.

These plants are apparently toxic and animals seem to be intuitively aware of this.

I crisscrossed the paddock, my excitement mounting steadily as I found one clump after another, as tightly packed as those I had found at the back of the shrubbery. Not all were daffodils. Some (more advanced) were obviously jonquils and some (a darker green) were probably snowflakes. They were all so close together that I was in constant danger of treading on them.

We had had daffodils in plenty round our little cottage in Golden Valley and I had supposed them to have been planted by an early owner when establishing the garden. But this paddock had clearly never been part of the garden. A tumbledown post-and-rail fence divided it from the cultivated garden and there were no trees or any other planting except for the hawthorn hedge that separated it from the lake paddock and one majestic old pear tree (a vision in spring) that had sown itself just outside the fence, on the road.

If there was such a profusion of daffodils in this paddock, then what might I not find all through the garden itself? I ran back, scaled the fence and started to search in earnest. I found them of course in their hundreds and thousands, under the big trees and lining the drive. In fact it became clear that they had once formed the border of the semicircular drive.

And I found them in the paddock on the other side of the drive beyond the hawthorn hedge, and in the paddock up behind the house, which had probably never formed part of the garden. When they flowered a few months later it was apparent that they were not all the same. Some were the common single yellow ones (if anything as lovely and as fragile looking as a daffodil can ever be called common), and there were lots of the crinkled old double ones found so often round deserted cottages and in paddocks where cottages have once been. I love these dearly. They were the kind that had been growing round the cottage in Golden Valley: mostly pure gold but often with a tinge of green.

But the daffodils at Forest Hall are of a great variety.

I also found a few patches of a double white, which I marked carefully with stones so that I would not lose track of them, thinking I might eventually move them into a garden bed for safe keeping. As well, I found single white ones, white ones with orange trumpets, pink ones (not many), and white ones with a deep orange line round the edge of the trumpet – probably the little Poeticus known as pheasant's eye. These surely had been

planted with intent, but they were not in rows or in beds, just scattered in the grass.

I thought of the daffodils in Alister Clark's garden at Glenara, on the slope opposite his house. Like these they were in a paddock that was not part of the garden – although it might once have been before fifty-odd years of neglect had taken their toll. After all it was at the top of this slope that Alister had built his marvellous stone folly, a tower that gave a bird's-eye view of the whole garden, as the tower at Sissinghurst does. Alister had bred daffodils as well as roses – hence the vast numbers and the great variety. Had someone bred them once at Forest Hall, I wondered.

I discovered from local people that Forest Hall is renowned for its daffodils and many make the trip to Deloraine in spring specially to see them. The paddock is clearly visible from the road so cars pull up, and tourists with cameras are almost a daily phenomenon. Some go further than taking photographs. They climb the fence to pick a bunch. But the numbers who did this dwindled rapidly once Joh and Willy arrived from Victoria. Blue heelers are notoriously territorial.

From one neighbour I heard a delightful story. Our predecessors had become not a little annoyed about trespassers trampling and picking the daffodils. So one year they decided (presumably in the absence of blue heelers) to put the bull in the daffodil paddock. He was a huge

Opposite above That first year we discovered daffodils and jonquils blooming far outside the garden, in the paddocks where cattle graze. *Opposite below left* It must have been the hand of a true gardener that planted fritillarias under one of the red hawthorns on the drive. *Opposite below right* There were many varieties of daffodils as well as snowflakes and jonquils.

Hereford and certainly looked intimidating. In reality he was a sleepy old creature but they felt he would be a decided deterrent. The very next day there was a knock on the front door and there stood a charming young couple who asked, ever so courteously, if the owners would mind moving the bull as they wanted to pick some daffodils!

There were no stormwater drains when we came to Forest Hall. The rain water simply emptied itself from the downpipes into the garden. We decided to install underground pipes to carry the stormwater right across the paddocks to the lake. So a man with a ditch-witch was employed to come in and dig trenches for the pipes. As he dug he left behind him a trail of disinterred bulbs. I could not bear to lose any of them, despite their vast number, so the dogs and I went along behind the machine, picking up the bulbs as he threw them up. This was a source of great entertainment to the builders who were working on the house, daffodils being to them almost in the nature of a weed. We replanted them later in the oak paddock.

There were other bulbs too, but not in such profusion as the daffodils. Under the two big cedars in the front is a carpet of English bluebells, and all over the garden, especially round the house, are patches of muscari. Beneath a crooked scarlet hawthorn is a tiny clump of the intriguing checked *Fritillaria meleagris*. Things such as this do not come about through chance seeding. Someone had gardened here lovingly and knowledgeably. Under a huge bay laurel on the edge of the sunny courtyard pink and white nerines came up, not in tens and twenties but in hundreds.

A long line of naked ladies (*Amaryllis belladonna*) in the grass that does duty for a lawn in front of the house had multiplied to such an extent and become so compacted that many of them no longer flowered. Sophisticated gardeners look down on these old pink lilies. They are so tough and hardy and flower in such humble gardens and such improbable places. There is nothing special, nothing exclusive about them at all. (Only the white ones are rare enough to be almost acceptable.) Yet I once visited the old cottage at Woolmers Estate, near Longford, at the right time of the year and found the circular drive lined with these despised pink lilies in full flower, hundreds of them. It was a sight not to be forgotten. Dividing ours to encourage them to flower again would be a task for the future.

Scilla peruviana came up just outside the back door – white ones as well as the more

34

frequently seen deep violet blue. Because of their name I thought – along with a lot of other gardeners, I suspect – that these lovely things had their origin in Peru. In fact they come from the Mediterranean and they do very well in our temperate climate.

Because they love our cold winters and mild summers I have added more bulbs, especially (non-artificial) tulips. It was twenty years ago in the garden of Eve Murray in Central Victoria that I first became aware of the dramatic impact of scarlet tulips in the spring landscape. Eve grew them with muscari among the daffodils she bred. I had gone home from a visit to her garden and sent off an order for them. But at that stage I tended to plant in tens and twenties. With a canvas such as we had at Forest Hall it was necessary to think bigger. So this time I sought out a Tasmanian grower and sent off an order for 2000 bulbs.

Judith Bowden lives on a splendid property near Bothwell. It is essentially a sheep property, but when the bottom fell out of the wool market Judith decided that tulips would be a possible sideline. I think it was as much a love affair as a business venture. After all people have been falling in love with tulips since the seventeenth century when tulipomania swept Europe, causing people to sacrifice even their homes to acquire these exotic flowers.

So from Judith I acquired my 2000 tulips – all 'Scarlet Apeldoorn' for the same colour makes a greater impact than twenty of this and twenty of that. The following year I visited the tulip farm at Table Cape on the north-east coast of Tasmania. The tulips were in flower, row upon row of them. I ordered huge golden ones appropriately named 'Big Smile', a sophisticated greenish white one called 'Maureen' and a low-growing, late-flowering, double pink one called 'Angélique'.

I love the species tulips, especially *Tulipa saxatilis*, which comes from Crete. It is low growing – to not much more than 15 centimetres – so ideal for growing under roses. The cup-shaped blooms are a soft lilac pink, with a golden throat. It multiplies quickly by underground stolons. I saw a mass of this little tulip one year in the garden at Buda, a historic house in Castlemaine, Victoria. They had become naturalised among the bluebells under the trees and the effect was entrancing. When mine have multiplied sufficiently I shall put some among the bluebells under the big cedars.

The bulbs, many of them a legacy of who knows which early owner, are without doubt one of the glories of the garden. From mid-August until the end of October, when the roses take over, they are a daily delight. But lovely as they are, they have presented me with my biggest design problem. Especially the daffodils.

Bounded on the south-west by the Bass Highway, on the south-east by a tall hawthorn hedge, on the north-west by the post-and-rail fence and on the north-east by a tumbledown stone wall impregnated by blackberry, the daffodil paddock was obviously no part of the original garden. How to make it appear so was a problem to which I devoted many hours of thought.

A sunny courtyard

ONE OF THE BASIC tenets of landscape architecture is that gardeners design their gardens on paper before they ever turn the first sod. Unfortunately it is something I have never been able to compel myself to do – possibly because I simply can't draw. So when I started to get to work on this garden, with its long-established trees and shrubs, I had really no idea where the boundaries of the garden might ultimately be, how much I would be able to maintain.

One thing was obvious: I would need some help – at least with the mowing. So I called in one morning to the local garage. Garage proprietors are an unfailing source of local knowledge. They know everybody in the town and they know everybody's business. I explained what I needed.

'Yes,' said Kevin promptly. 'We'll send John Wilson out.'

The next day a car came to a stop on the drive – a canary-yellow car pulling a large trailer encouragingly full of tools. When John Wilson got out I was appalled to see that he had only one leg. How could he ever manage to mow an area as large as this?

'It's a very big garden,' I said tentatively.

'I can do it,' came the answer.

'And the edges will all need doing with the brush cutter.'

'I can do that too,' he said.

He has done it ever since. He can't use a ride-on mower. He gets along on his crutches and pushes the mower with his chest. He does the edges in the same way. He

The acid green of *Euphorbia characias* subsp. *wulfenii* on a corner at the back of the house is in stark contrast to the dark red of a dahlia that makes its appearance unbidden each year. *Opposite above* A stone figure nestles under the branches of *Rosa* 'Dupontii' on the arch in the sunny courtyard. *Opposite below* John arrived when we needed someone to cut the lawns, but has become an expert in the art of constructing dry-stone walls.

does them splendidly. He is unfailingly cheerful and absolutely reliable. He has never told me he can't do something. He has never complained of being tired. I think he loves the garden. He makes a special trip out here if we are expecting garden visitors, to make sure it looks its best. He has become a true friend.

John comes one day a week, sometimes two. I wish I had him twice as often. He is invaluable.

I decided to start from the house and work outwards. Because it faces south-west, it gets little morning sun; however, the sheltered grassy courtyard behind it is warm and bathed in sunshine for a good part of the day. A perfect place for roses.

The courtyard is bounded by the back wall of the house, a wall of the kitchen and adjoining dairy and, across the other side of the drive, the blacksmith's cottage. This, I decided, would be the place to start.

It was, and still is, dominated by a magnificent blue wisteria that runs the full length of the kitchen and dairy and is inextricably bound up with a huge bush of the old Tea rose 'Fortune's Double Yellow', one of only six roses we found when we moved to Forest Hall. Both the wisteria and the rose have trunks like tree trunks and must be over a hundred years old. In early spring the combination of the blue of the wisteria and the strange apricot gold of 'Fortune's Double Yellow' is a sight to behold.

I never cease to be thankful to Robert Fortune, who brought this rose to England from China in 1845. It must have come to Australia not much later for it is found in many early Australian gardens. It is a wild, recalcitrant old fellow who bitterly resents being pruned or trained. Fortunately for ours I don't think anyone had ever so much as shown it the secateurs for many, many years so it has wound its way up through the wisteria and emerged triumphant high above the roof.

Rose Kingsley, writing in 1907 in *Eversley Gardens and Others*, described 'Fortune's Double Yellow' as 'a source of pride and delight to its happy possessor'. She had 'vivid recollections of its exquisite effect tumbling over a high grey stone wall by the dusty roadside from Genoa to Pegli . . . and each year from the ground to the roof it is showered over with scores of lovely blossoms . . . it is without exception the most cruelly prickly thorny Rose I know – every dainty twig, every shiny leaf being armed with ferocious fish-hooks.' Perhaps this explains why ours had never been pruned. It was this rose that determined the colour scheme for the whole courtyard. As a precaution I added a plant of the much more amenable Noisette rose 'Cloth of Gold' in case 'Fortune's Double Yellow' should ever succumb to old age.

Outside the back door is a lilac – not a sophisticated rare variety but the ordinary everyday lilac that is found in most old gardens. I'm sure I could find a more exciting variety but so far I haven't had the heart to replace it.

A stone-flagged path leads straight from this door to the drive; where the two meet, someone years ago had planted, parallel to the back wall of the house, a cotoneaster hedge. This had grown to giant proportions and succeeded in excluding much of the sun from the courtyard. I don't harbour the same dislike for cotoneaster that I do for the ubiquitous photinia, but there are much more attractive hedges. A single plant of cotoneaster can be appealing when smothered in tiny white flowers or scarlet berries, but a row of ten to fifteen is uninteresting to say the least. It had to go.

It was tough and the root system a tangled mass. Removing it was quite beyond my capabilities. So I called in a young local nurseryman, Peter Cooper, and he, after two days of hard labour and with the help of our old four-wheel drive, finally managed to remove it.

When it was gone a series of short metal posts indicated that there had once been a fence there. The following year another one-time owner sent us some photographs taken in the 1940s and there was a neat white-painted picket fence where the cotoneaster had been. The fence was certainly preferable to the cotoneaster but I didn't want either. What I wanted was a fairly low-growing rose hedge. The drive was one step higher than the path so I decided to try a two-tiered hedge. For the top level I chose 'Bloomfield Dainty' – a pale yellow flushed with apricot, which fades to white. The colour was right, the height was right and, while it hates the cold in England, it would love the warm conditions in this courtyard. On the lower level I planted David Austin's 'Wildflower'. Like 'Bloomfield Dainty' it bears single flowers. They are a pale creamy yellow and the foliage, again similar to that of 'Bloomfield Dainty', is small and glossy. They would be perfect companions.

I read in *Botanica's Roses* that 'Wildflower' has been left off many growers' lists and is rarely grown mainly because it is, like many yellow roses, susceptible to black spot. So

is 'Bloomfield Dainty' but the two together are so charming that I am prepared to forgive them – and even to treat them to an occasional dose of Triforine if absolutely necessary.

The corner where the wall of the house meets the wall of the kitchen I reserved for the temperamental 'Gloire de Dijon' – a pale buff-shaded apricot. I had grown her at Bleak House and for the first couple of years she had lived up to her name and was a glory indeed. Then came a series of colder than usual winters and she sulked and refused to perform. She is a daughter of the exquisite temperamental unreliable 'Souvenir de la Malmaison' and has inherited all her parent's faults. Perfect flowers are rare. Often they turn brown and mushy in the bud. I had almost given her up. But here was the perfect spot – warm, sunny, protected. I decided to give her one last chance. So she was given the prime spot and I am hoping she will take advantage of it. She is capable at her best of becoming the 'Glory of Forest Hall'.

In the same bed, under the dining-room window, I planted one of my favourite Tea roses, 'Jean Ducher'. She loves it here. Her ivory-coloured blooms, flushed palest apricot and with a delicious Tea scent, nod in the window all through summer, and in 2000 as late as early July. I once saw a plant of 'Jean Ducher' in the hotter climate of Western Australia. It reached to the top of a 3-metre-high fence and flowered all through winter.

I was fortunate to find a plant of a delightful China rose, 'Comtesse du Cayla', just before I read about her in Vita Sackville-West's book *A Joy of Gardening*. She was described as 'somewhat romantic in her associations, for the lady in whose honour she is named was mistress of Louis XVIII'. This was incentive enough to win her a place in the garden but on a more practical level Vita Sackville-West wrote that she is 'altogether a desirable rose not liable to black spot or mildew; needing little pruning apart from the removal of wood when it has become too old, say, every two or three years'. And the colour was right – a coppery apricot. I went straight back to the nursery and bought a second plant.

Opposite The tall modern rose 'Sutter's Gold' (left) and Alister Clark's 'Squatter's Dream' (far right) were chosen to harmonise with 'Fortune's Double Yellow', which weaves its way up through the wisteria on the far left.

And while I was there I came across another little China rose I have not grown before – 'Arethusa'. The flowers are a pale pinky apricot and she is described in one of the French *Journal des Roses* as being 'of the Queen Mab sort'. I found later that she is named for the nymph who inhabits the spring of Arethusa, near Syracuse in Sicily. She flowers generously and has earned her place in the garden.

Right under the window of the room we call the red room, where we can enjoy its fragrance every day, I planted 'Marie van Houtte' – the colour of clotted cream with suggestions of pink. And here too I found space for a couple of David Austin's English Roses – 'Jaquenetta' for the delicately scented, almost single, palest apricot blooms, although it has the reputation of being 'unreliable in its repeat bloom' (*Botanica's Roses*), and 'Windrush' for its semi-single, pale creamy yellow flowers and wonderful fragrance – it is totally reliable and bred from two of my all-time favourites, 'Canterbury' and 'Golden Wings'.

It was Ethel Turner, whose books were my generation's childhood favourites, who wrote in *The Ungardeners* that 'unless you know the people who own the garden . . . it will not be a garden at all but just a piece of land containing flowerbeds'. In the same way plants assume a special significance, an extra dimension for us if we have some connection with the people for whom they were named. And so, for me, the small early-Australian-bred Tea rose 'Penelope' is very special for it was named for a dearly loved cousin. It bears creamy white flowers marked with dark red – enough cream to fit my colour scheme and little enough dark red not to jar. I planted three and am reminded of Penelope Corrie almost every day.

At the end of this bed is the indispensable downpipe – plastic and therefore not approved of by the Heritage people, or by me for that matter. I have planted at its foot the superb, understandably popular, vivid apricot 'Crépuscule'. I don't know how far up the downpipe she will climb but in any case her beauty is such that it will ensure that all eyes are for her alone.

I was running out of space but I could not omit in this symphony of gold and apricot some of my favourites. So on the path leading from the back door to the drive I planted three each of dear old reliable, fragrant, creamy 'Safrano', heavenly scented, golden 'Lady

Hillingdon' and the single apricot 'Mrs Oakley Fisher'. And on the other side of the path Alister Clark's 'Squatter's Dream' – a mystery rose this one, from an unknown seedling crossed with a seedling of *Rosa gigantea*. Alister was often not very particular about recording his crosses. This rose is a charmer – rich gold, flushed with apricot, and single, not unlike 'Mrs Oakley Fisher'. It has virtually no thorns and is continually in flower.

At the end of the same path I found space for two plants of 'Howard Florey', a rose from the fine Australian breeder George Thomson. Its brilliant apricot colouring and wavy petals are reminiscent of the popular 'Just Joey'. It was released in 1999 to celebrate the centenary of the birth of the outstanding Australian scientist who was awarded the Nobel Prize for Medicine in 1945 for his work in developing penicillin. The rose is a beauty and flowers nearly as generously as 'Squatter's Dream'. It is the result of a cross between two very well-loved roses – 'Apricot Nectar' and 'Seduction'.

On the north corner of the courtyard I have erected a wide arch leading onto the drive and on each side of it I have planted the superb single white 'Dupontii', which is equally happy treated as a climber or as a large shrub.

Underplanting could wait. But bulbs came up in their thousands. Bluebells formed a carpet where I had planted 'Crépuscule'. Jonquils came into flower as early as the end of July, and the paths were thickly lined with the deep blue of muscari. At the back door was the patch of *Scilla peruviana*, and under the laurel hundreds of pink and white nerines. The latter didn't fit the colour scheme at all and bit by bit I have moved them to other parts of the garden. But a tenacious species gladiolus – I think it is *G. communis* subsp. *byzantinus* – absolutely refuses to be discouraged and continues to thrust its magenta-pink spires up among the apricot roses each summer.

Then just as I thought this section of the garden was satisfactorily catered for, I came upon the story of Julia Clements.

⊶═⊷

The importance of a name

I HAD GROWN 'Julia's Rose' in Victoria in a bed devoted to a group of strange coffee-coloured roses popular with flower arrangers and interior decorators. There I had 'Café' and 'Lavender Pinocchio' (thought to have been an early attempt at a blue rose) and 'Julia's Rose'. Regularly I picked her lovely milk-coffee-coloured blooms to fill a bowl on the dining-room table, loving their reflection in the polished wood.

But for a long time, although I loved and cherished her rose, I had no idea who Julia might be. Then in an antiquarian bookshop I found a volume called *My Life with Flowers* by Julia Clements. It turned out to be the autobiography of one of the most famous floral artists of the century. And it was for her that Tysterman in 1976 named this lovely rose, a cross between 'Blue Moon' and 'Dr A. J. Verhage'.

Reading of Julia's life, of her travels to exotic places, it is tempting to conclude that here was a privileged woman who led a life of comfort and ease. Nothing could be further from the truth. In fact Julia took up flower arranging at the end of World War II because she saw that flowers could bring joy into the lives of women saddened and depressed and

---

Opposite 'Julia's Rose' is aptly named for a flower arranger. Its strange milk-coffee-coloured blooms have ensured its continuing popularity with designers.

exhausted after long years of struggle and deprivation. Her own experiences during the war had been horrendous.

In one year, 1945, her London home had been bombed and demolished, her husband reported missing believed killed, and her baby born dead during an air raid when there had been no doctor at hand and no blood available for transfusions. It was her love of flowers that carried her through and gave new meaning to her life. 'Flowers,' she wrote, 'are a universal language, understood by all no matter what race or colour or creed, and they spread love and beauty to all those who work with them.'

And so began a life of travel, centred around the talks and demonstrations Julia gave worldwide. She tells of her first tour to the USA shortly after the end of the war. Clothes were rationed in Britain and she had nothing smart to wear when she had to stand in front of wealthy and sophisticated audiences relatively untouched by war. Having no clothing coupons left, she pulled down her lace curtains to make a blouse, and set off.

From the outset her talks were a success. She was invited to garden clubs all over the world and was responsible for founding many new clubs. She tells of visits to Monet's garden at Giverny, to the chapel of St Fiacre, the patron saint of gardeners, in Brittany, of her meeting with Mother Teresa in Calcutta. She writes of judging flowers at the Chelsea Flower Show, and of her trip each year to the great rose festival staged by the National Rose Society at St Albans where one can see some 30 000 roses of all varieties in 21 acres of garden.

The Royal Horticultural Society awarded Julia Clements their highest honour, the Victoria Medal of Honour, for her work with flower clubs, and in 1989 she was awarded the OBE. Looking back on her life, she concludes that her work with flowers has led many women to be more aware of beauty and of nature and has provided a creative outlet for many who had neither the means nor opportunity to pursue a study of the arts.

No wonder that Tysterman gave her name to this lovely rose. She has had other roses named after her – 'Julia Clements' and 'Lady Seton' (her second marriage was to Sir Alexander Seton but he lived for only six months afterwards and Julia turned again to flowers for consolation). I have never seen these two roses in Australia; however, having read her story, I was determined to find a place for 'Julia's Rose' in my garden. It belonged of course in the sunny courtyard with all the buff and apricot roses, although there was now an acute shortage of room.

Beside the back door, on the other side from the lilac, was a poor crippled rose that, despite its frailty, still bore a steady succession of powerfully fragrant, deepest wine-red blooms. I had felt for some time that it could not stay there. The colour was wrong and the plant anything but beautiful. I had been pondering its future at the time when we were given the history of Forest Hall and the Bonnily family. In this was a photograph of Annie Bonnily, the wife of the second William Bonnily. She was pictured standing outside the door, dressed in black, her white hair drawn severely back. And beside her was the rose – large and flourishing at that time but unmistakably the same rose. It must have stood there for a hundred years or so. I wondered how many women had picked its velvety blooms and stopped to smell its scent as they passed through the door. This rose was a part of the history of Forest Hall. I could not simply dig it out and cast it aside.

But if I did take it out I would have the perfect place for 'Julia's Rose'. So from the spindly branches I took cuttings. I could only get seven but I gave them my best care and attention. They spent the winter in the glasshouse and the following spring I potted up seven sturdy little plants. I had at that time no idea what I was going to do with them.

Neither did I have any idea what this old rose might be. I remembered the wise words of the American rose expert and writer Brent Dickerson, who wrote that 'identification of roses old or new is an intricate and demanding affair, and one should begin any attempt with the clear understanding that success is unlikely'. Alister Clark, I feel sure, would have entirely agreed with him. I remembered his asking someone who presented him with a basket of tired blooms that they wanted identified whether people realised that to date (it was 1940) over 11 000 different roses had been imported into Australia and he had not seen a fraction of them. And how much greater the number would be today, so many years on.

I thought too of the table often set aside at rose conferences for unknown roses in the hope that the 'experts' will be able to name them. I have seen towards the end of a conference as many as a dozen names attached to one rose.

But it is tempting to try! At least with my red rose I had, because of the photograph, an approximate date to go by – not the date of release of course, but at least the certainty of its having been in the garden at the time the photograph was taken. Annie Bonnily had lived from 1846 to 1931. She looks in her photograph to have been in her sixties. So the rose may have been there around the turn of the twentieth century.

At first sight I had thought it could have been the marvellous dark red 'Château de Clos Vougeot'. It had the same sprawly habit of growth, the rather sparse foliage and the rich scent. 'Château de Clos Vougeot' had been released by Pernet-Ducher of France in 1908, by which time Annie would have been in her sixties. If it had come fairly promptly from France to Australia it is just possible that this battered old warrior was indeed 'Château de Clos Vougeot'.

This is my best guess. But from such scanty unscientific anecdotal evidence little can be deduced with any certainty. So I shall continue to call it Annie's rose. The important thing is that these old roses should be preserved and tended in order to give pleasure to future gardeners.

Accordingly, after the addition of several barrows of new topsoil, 'Julia's Rose' was established in the prime position beside the door, and the cuttings from Annie's rose were relegated to the glasshouse pending the discovery of the perfect place for them.

Annie Bonnily.

The blacksmith's cottage

ONLY THE DRIVE and a strip of garden separate the blacksmith's cottage, with its dirt floor and walls of split shingles, from the sunny courtyard. It is surprising that this quaint little building – the sort of building a child might draw, with a door in the centre and a window on each side – was allotted a position of such prominence. Apart from the house, it is the first building you see as you follow the drive around, and it is visible from all the windows at the back of the house.

But then the blacksmith was a very important member of the establishment. Horses were vital – they pulled both the coach and the plough. They were used for riding and hunting so the blacksmith was in constant demand. William Bonnily trained as a blacksmith, the family records tell us, before he left his native Scotland. I imagined him with his sturdy frame and long white beard standing at the forge, 'big-boned and hardy-handsome' like Hopkins's Felix Randal the farrier, who did 'fettle for the great grey drayhorse his bright and battering sandal'. And the forge is still there complete with its huge bellows and still able to be used – if anyone knew how to.

The little cottage is dominated by a giant yew shaped like a drum, which stands at the south end of the wall facing the kitchen. The yew introduces a note of formality not found anywhere else in the garden. When all else had been so obviously neglected the yew had – equally obviously – been the pride of the garden, carefully tended, regularly clipped. It reaches to the top of the roof, where it is then cut sheer across, and it measures some 4 metres in diameter.

At the opposite end of the cottage we found a pair of ancient lilacs, a flourishing bush of the egg-yolk yellow *Kerria japonica* and a rampant jasmine, *Jasminum polyanthum*, with its pink buds and deliciously scented white flowers. All of these, so beloved by last century's gardeners, we have left. The front of the building was clothed in Virginia creeper (*Parthenocissus quinquefolia*) – a wonderful sight in autumn – and at the door was an untamed bush of *Spiraea cantoniensis* so big that it made getting through the door difficult and sometimes impossible.

The cottage is set about 8 metres back from the drive and the area between was given over to rough grass, sticky Willy, docks and dandelions, with a second spiraea placed dead centre and surrounded by a symmetrical concrete border. Who from the many generations of gardeners was responsible for this I could not conjecture – clearly not the one who had left the fine legacy of trees. Without doubt this was the next place to tackle. The spiraea and the concrete were removed – not without difficulty – and the 'lawn' subjected to a couple of strong doses of Round-up.

We did not touch the building. If it has stood for close on 150 years no doubt it will stand for a few more. And it is, like Annie's old red rose, part of the history of Forest Hall. It makes, moreover, a splendid potting shed. Although the forge and bellows remain in place, the strong wooden benches now house an assortment of hand tools and labels, propagating hormone, fertilisers, potting mix and plastic pots. One day, I hope, the tools will be hung neatly on the walls, each one in its place, as I remember seeing them in the toolshed at Joan Law-Smith's garden, Bolobek, the outline of each tool etched in black on the white walls. At the moment this is the stuff that dreams are made of.

Because it is visible from the sunny courtyard, the colour scheme chosen for the cottage needed to harmonise with the colours used there. Consequently I surrounded it initially with some of my best-loved yellow roses. Adjacent to the drive I planted three 'Buff

Opposite In the blacksmith's garden 'Claire Jacquier' and 'Céline Forestier' are supported by a three-sided arch. The blue jar echoes the colour of the roof and of the muscari that carpet this garden in early spring.

Beauty', three 'Leverkusen' and three 'Maigold'. All of these can be treated either as large shrubs or as climbers. While 'Buff Beauty' and 'Maigold' are favourites with many gardeners, 'Leverkusen' has never achieved the respect and attention it merits, I think. It is a Kordesii hybrid and produces its double, clear yellow flowers through much of the summer. The small, dark green, glossy leaves are attractive in their own right. To these roses I added one plant of 'Bloomfield Dainty' – an insurance in case I lost one of the plants in the courtyard hedge and needed to replace it. Like many forms of insurance, this has fortunately (so far) proved unnecessary.

David Austin's English Roses do extraordinarily well in the cool-temperate climate of Tasmania, so I added two each of pale yellow 'The Pilgrim', glowing 'Golden Celebration' and – for me and I suspect for many others – the best of his yellows, the truly splendid 'Graham Thomas'. I would have planted it in any case as a tribute to its namesake, but for such a very beautiful rose no justification is needed.

With the abolition of the former 'lawn' I was left with an impossibly large raised bed, measuring some 30 metres by 8 metres: too big altogether, too difficult to work in, too difficult to control. An existing straight path, unfortunately in concrete, connected the drive to the door of the cottage. I decided to run a path through at right angles to it – a fairly narrow gravel path just wide enough to take a barrow.

On each side of the gravel path – well back – I planted three of the glorious spinosissima (or pimpinellifolia) hybrid 'Frühlingsgold', well named for it is one of the earliest to flower, and is truly a herald of the spring. These have grown in four years into huge shrubs and are a source of real joy. To them I added their relative 'Frühlingsduft', a creamy yellow flushed with pink. Both of these superb roses have as one parent the Hybrid Tea 'Joanna Hill', which I have never seen.

I planted another of my favourite yellows, 'Golden Wings', on either side of the door. This too is a spinosissima hybrid, crossed with another yellow Hybrid Tea, 'Soeur Thérèse'. It, unlike the others, is recurrent and we enjoy its single golden blooms all through summer.

I never can have sufficient climbers. For it is they that lend a garden that air of romance and mystery. The walls of the little blacksmith's cottage were almost covered already with the Virginia creeper, the yew, the jasmine and the lilacs. But at the south corner I found room for just one climber and decided on the striking 'Lawrence Johnston', named for the creator of the great garden at Hidcote. I am looking forward to the time when it will, as one English rosarian, Jack Harkness, assures us in his book *Roses*, turn the wall into 'a sheet of gold'. I love this rose. I love its single, pure gold flowers against the rough shingle wall. I love the association with Hidcote. I hope it will climb quickly to the roof of the cottage and mingle with the dark green of the yew and the soft blue of the clematis 'Will Goodwin' that I have planted at the rose's feet.

Soon after, I came upon a pretty three-sided arch, which I erected at the other end of this big bed. It opened the door for three more climbers and I spent a long time making my choice. I find the Noisettes among the most rewarding of roses and I settled finally on one plant of 'Claire Jacquier' and two plants of 'Céline Forestier'. 'Céline Forestier' was bred in 1858, some thirty years earlier than 'Claire Jacquier'. Both are pale yellow, fading to cream. Graham Thomas writes in his *Rose Book* of 'Céline Forestier' that she has 'a spicy Tea rose fragrance, powerful, delicious and intense'. He also notes that she can be slow to establish but once happy is constantly in flower. 'Claire Jacquier' is described in *Modern Roses XI* as being of very vigorous growth and 'possibly *R. multiflora* × Tea rose'.

Both of these descriptions have been borne out in my garden. 'Céline Forestier' has been slow of growth, while 'Claire Jacquier' has romped to the top of the arch like a true multiflora, crossed over, and is threatening to dominate the whole thing. A large-flowered, deep violet-blue clematis, 'Daniel Deronda', has proved to be the perfect companion for her.

Then when I thought I had definitely finished with climbers in this bed, I came upon an exceptionally healthy plant of 'Phyllis Bide' and could not resist her. The result of a cross between those two splendid roses 'Perle d'Or' and 'Gloire de Dijon', she bears enchanting little pale yellow flowers, flushed with pink and apricot. So I bought a tripod for her, which I think will be a sufficient support. And beside her I put two (cutting-grown) plants of 'Perle d'Or'. This must be surely one of the hardiest of roses. I have found her in almost every old Tasmanian garden I have visited. My cuttings this time came from a deserted 1830s stone farmhouse in the Meander Valley, called Old Wesley Dale. Most of the garden

'Lawrence Johnston' and the lavender-blue clematis 'Will Goodwin'
climb up the pine lattice on the wall of the blacksmith's cottage, and
the deep blue of nepetas and the scarlet of the geum 'Mrs Bradshaw'
add a contrasting note. On the left is the recurrent-flowering
'Golden Wings'.

here was gone except for a few hoary trees. But 'Perle d'Or' near the back door was covered in blooms. I had no secateurs and no knife so had to break off a few little pieces with my fingers. Every mutilated piece struck.

The more roses one grows, the more interested one becomes in the fascinating absorbing perplexing history of this sentimentally named queen of flowers. I want to include in the Forest Hall garden those roses that have played a special role, made an outstanding contribution to the history of the rose. But above all I want a beautiful garden. So while I wish to include these often strange old roses in my planting, the first and foremost consideration is aesthetic.

It would be difficult to overestimate the historic importance of the four roses commonly known as 'the stud Chinas' for the China rose is, in the words of Graham Thomas, 'the foundation species upon which all our modern roses are built'. Hence in the bed of yellow roses I wanted to include 'Parks' Yellow Tea-scented China', the rose that gave us such treasures as 'Gloire de Dijon' and 'Maréchal Niel'. It is not easy to grow, especially in England, and it is not a spectacular flower, but I wanted to give it a try.

At the end of this long yellow bed, on the south-east side of the blacksmith's garden, I had planted a group of trees – four *Amelanchier canadensis* and two *Prunus padus*, the bird cherry – to screen it from the predominantly pink bed that was to be planted beyond. The amelanchier is surely one of the loveliest of small ornamental trees, with its froth of white flowers in spring, its strange pinkish fawn foliage and its brilliant autumn colour. At the foot of the trees I planted two of 'Parks' Yellow Tea-scented China'. So far they are doing well, thrusting long arms up into the lower branches of the trees. And this spring they flowered better than I ever expected that they would.

Also important in the history of yellow roses is *R. hemisphaerica*. It is one of the earliest yellow roses in cultivation, having been grown prior to 1625. And although its strange cupped, sulphur-yellow flowers often ball, turn brown and fail to open properly (shades of 'Souvenir de la Malmaison'), it is worth growing for its foliage alone and for the odd good flower it produces. The leaves are delicately formed and a soft pale green. They are described by John Parkinson in *Paradisi in Sole: Paradisus Terrestris* (1629) as being 'finely snipt about the edges' and the bark of the young shoots as being 'of a sad greene reddish colour'. It seems to lose its leaves very late, and I have planted underneath it twenty or thirty *Tigridia pavonia*, the peacock flower. They provide colour – brilliant reds and yellows – to compensate for the paucity of flowers on *R. hemisphaerica*.

Then there is 'Soleil d'Or' of which Graham Thomas wrote that 'the bulk of our flame and orange modern roses have this rose in their ancestry'. Bred in 1900 by Pernet-Ducher, one of its parents was the Persian Yellow Rose. The colour is rich yellow-shaded orange, a triumph for its breeder who had sought for many years to breed a yellow rose that would be remontant. There have been more conflicting opinions regarding 'Soleil d'Or' than almost any other rose. They range from ecstatic to downright condemnatory. But there can be no doubt at all about its importance in the history of the rose.

I grew it in Victoria – not very successfully. It was plagued by black spot as some of its critics said it would be, and it flowered sparsely. Here in Tasmania it promises better things. I planted two and lost one. But the survivor is excelling itself and last summer it bore some splendid blooms on long arching canes. It still suffers from black spot but I think it has settled in, and I am looking forward to its next performance. Under it I have planted a prostrate powder-blue ceanothus, *C. gloriosus* 'Emily Brown', and put prostrate rosemary in the raised planter box built onto the wall behind it.

The low-growing 'Gold Bunny' has been planted to edge the gravel path, together with the lemon-yellow 'Moonsprite' and masses of the bulbous blue Dutch iris 'Professor Blaauw'.

A collection of geums (scarlet 'Mrs Bradshaw', vivid orange *G. × borisii*), potentillas (*P. aurea*, *P. fruticosa* 'Red Ace' and bronze *P. × tonguei*) and nepetas (*N. × faassenii*, 'Six Hills Giant', 'Walker's Blue' and *N. nervosa*) have been used as underplantings with species gladioli and masses of the little tulip *Tulipa saxatilis*. The path from the drive to the door of the cottage is thickly lined with muscari, and the scarlet tulips later in the spring are spectacular.

By now I felt that this bed was more or less under control – then I found a plant of the forsythia known as 'Beatrix Farrand'. I had just finished reading the fascinating account of her life written by Jane Brown. It was called simply *Beatrix*, with a sub-title *The Gardening Life of Beatrix Jones Farrand*.

Previously Beatrix Farrand had been little more than a name to me. By the time I had

'Buff Beauty' (left) and 'Leverkusen' (far right) are among the
yellow roses in the blacksmith's garden. In the background is the
evergreen dogwood *Cornus capitata*.

finished the book and read of her relationship to Edith Wharton (she was her niece), her close friendship with Henry James, her invaluable work in laying out the gardens at Dartington Hall in England, and at Dumbarton Oaks, Harvard and Yale universities and the White House in the USA, and of her foresight in collecting and preserving the drawings of Gertrude Jekyll, I had some concept of the stature of this astonishing woman. So I found a place for 'Beatrix Farrand' behind 'Maigold', where it bursts into flower in early spring before most of the roses have their first buds and while the scarlet tulips are still flowering, and I pick long sprays to fill the dining room with sunshine.

It is plants such as this, with associations such as this, that add another dimension to our gardens. Dorothy Elmhirst had not been a gardener until she came under the influence of Beatrix Farrand and started to be involved in the garden at Dartington Hall. I love the letter that Beatrix wrote to Dorothy's husband, Leonard: 'Tell Dorothy with my dearest love that no one ever starts gardening too late or too early, once it gets into one's blood it can never get out . . . so she must resign herself for the rest of her days to be constantly struggling and constantly enjoying her garden.'

Three sports and a foundling

THE FOUNDLING CAME first. I saw it listed in the catalogue of Ross Roses, South Australia, and loved the description: old Tea rose, many petalled and with typical old Tea rose scent. It grows, so the description read, to a huge bush and flowers constantly – big, flat flowers the colour of clotted cream, sometimes tinged with pink.

It had been found in the old cemetery at Blakiston in South Australia. No one knew its name so it was given the name on the grave where it was growing – 'Octavius Weld'. The date on the tombstone suggested that this lovely rose had made its way to Australia some time in the late nineteenth century. Maureen Ross saw it and was responsible for propagating and registering it.

I spent a fascinating couple of hours in the cemetery a few years ago when I was researching *Rose Gardens of Australia*. It was one of the few cemeteries Simon Griffiths, the photographer, and I found, in our search for old roses, that had not been 'tidied up'. The roses were growing untramelled and unrestrained, tumbling over the gravestones and weaving their way through the iron railings and up into trees. So when I saw the listing and provenance of 'Octavius Weld' it brought back such happy memories that I had to have it.

I didn't really have room for it among the yellows and apricots of the blacksmith's garden but this was where it belonged, so in the end I popped it in behind 'Buff Beauty' and I'm hoping for the best. If it grows as big as the description suggests, one or the other – or both – will have to be rigorously pruned. To date it has been slow to take off. Perhaps next spring?

Palest apricot yellow, 'Jean Galbraith' is a sport of the much deeper apricot 'Abraham Darby'. *Opposite above* 'Abraham Darby' himself. *Opposite below* Ravensworth, built in 1826, has given its name to a pale yellow sport of the apricot-coloured 'Perle d'Or'.

The first sport to arrive was 'Betsy Taaffe', a gift from David Taaffe, a Victorian nurseryman. He had found this soft yellow bloom on a bush of the vivid apricot rose 'Abraham Darby', which was growing in his garden. I had grown 'Abraham Darby' at Erinvale and was constantly amazed both by the size of the blooms and the number on the bush at any one time. It seemed to be constantly covered by huge, flat, very full, vibrant apricot flowers, with one of the strongest scents in the garden. The colour is described by David Austin, its breeder, as a 'coppery apricot'. One of his aims was to introduce new colours not found in the old European roses. With 'Abraham Darby' he certainly succeeded.

'Abraham Darby' is unusual among David Austin's English Roses in that its parents are both modern roses. One is the delightful many-petalled, mid-pink climber 'Aloha', and the other a yellow floribunda called 'Yellow Cushion', which I don't think I have ever seen. 'Abraham Darby' also has an unusual name for an English Rose. Where most of David Austin's roses are named for characters in English literature (Cymbeline, Othello, Prospero, Tess of the d'Urbervilles, Jude the Obscure) and some for famous people and places (Sir Edward Elgar, Tradescant, Canterbury, Constance Spry, John Clare), Abraham Darby was called after an industrialist, an iron master who founded the Bristol Iron Company in 1709. A strange choice of name for a rose.

'Betsy Taaffe' was named after David Taaffe's mother, who made a beautiful rose garden in New Zealand. The rose resembles its parent in most respects but the colour varies from soft apricot to lemon yellow. The scent is less strong than that of its parent but it has the ability, like 'Abraham Darby', to flower over a very long period, and like its parent it is also a good cut flower.

Then came 'Ravensworth'. As with 'Octavius Weld', I discovered it in Ross's catalogue and it was of particular interest to me because it had been found in an early Tasmanian garden and is a sport of the redoubtable 'Perle d'Or'. Only the colour is different. 'Ravensworth' is a soft creamy yellow. It is named for the house where it was found – one of those simple, dignified Georgian houses so characteristic of Tasmania. The house was built as early as 1826 and, like Forest Hall, is surrounded by ancient trees – oaks, cedars and maples, magnolias, sweet chestnuts and pears. The rose known as 'Ravensworth' is growing in dense shade under trees that meet overhead. The bush has grown huge, as

'Perle d'Or' does if given its freedom, and although there were no blooms on the day of my visit the spent heads told of a prolific harvest. The house had stayed in one family, as houses sometimes do in Tasmania, for over a hundred years. The present owners have lived and gardened there for twenty-eight years. 'Perle d'Or' had come to Ravensworth years ago as a cutting from a keen and knowledgeable gardener, Sheila Gee, a descendant of one of the early settlers.

I was given cuttings of 'Ravensworth'. They struck as readily as those of its parent do. For the first year I grew them in large pots at the back door. This was a rose I felt I could not do without and here there was no chance of the plants being neglected. This year I have allotted them a place in the blacksmith's garden near 'Perle d'Or' itself, and its other relative 'Phyllis Bide'.

Then last year when my annual parcel of roses from Nieuwesteeg's Rose Nursery in Melbourne arrived in early August, I was surprised to find included in it five (unsolicited) plants of a rose labelled 'Jean Galbraith'. Attached to them was a note from John Nieuwesteeg saying that this was a sport of the David Austin rose 'Abraham Darby' (that man again!), which had appeared on one of his bushes. He had propagated and registered it, and thought I might like to try it.

I was doubly pleased to receive this rose as I had just purchased a copy of the fascinating book *Kindred Spirits* by Anne Latreille. This will undoubtedly become a prized possession for many Australian gardeners as it is the story of a most unusual friendship based on a passionate love of gardens and plants. It is the story of the correspondence that passed between Jean Galbraith and Joan Law-Smith, the one a distinguished botanist, the other a fine botanical artist.

At the time this correspondence started Joan was living in the Western District of Victoria where, as well as helping on the property and bringing up three small children, she was making a garden. But her real ambition was to succeed as a botanical artist. She felt she lacked the scientific knowledge that is essential to all who would accurately depict plants. She had heard of Jean Galbraith. Perhaps she had read and enjoyed Jean's book *Garden in a Valley*, which had been published in 1939 and tells of the making of her own garden. Assuredly she had read and enjoyed Jean's articles in *Garden Lover* and the *Age*.

But Jean lived in Gippsland, in eastern Victoria, far removed from the Western District. This made personal contact difficult. However, these were two determined and resourceful women. They devised a plan whereby lessons were conducted by correspondence. Jean wrote her botany lessons, then sent them to Joan, who subsequently returned them with appropriate drawings.

In this way Joan gained the knowledge she required. Her own books bear testimony to this and there will be very many Australian gardeners who cherish *A Gardener's Diary*, written to impart basic gardening knowledge to her daughters, *The Uncommon Garden* and *Gardens of the Mind*, a collection of poems and extracts about gardens that were of significance to her. These three books are illustrated by Joan's own delicate and sensitive paintings of flowers and foliage, birds and mice and ladybirds. Lastly Joan published in 1991 *The Garden Within*, which traces the life of Bolobek, the exquisitely restrained and tranquil garden she made at the foot of Mt Macedon, and takes the reader through the garden season by season. This book is illustrated not by paintings but by superb photographs that show the garden in all its detail, all its moods. Jean's love was more for Australian native plants than for introduced ones, as reflected in her books *Wildflowers of Victoria* and *A Field Guide to the Wildflowers of South-East Australia*.

Joan created a secluded walled rose garden at Bolobek that became for some visitors the heart of the garden. Most of the roses there are old European roses – 'Mme Hardy', 'Celeste', *R. alba* 'Maxima', 'Boule de Neige', 'Mme Pierre Oger', 'Reine des Violettes' – although David Austin's 'Constance Spry' is espaliered against the mellow walls, and I feel sure that Joan would rejoice to know that a beautiful rose has been named for Jean and would certainly have found a place for it too in her garden.

It was *Garden in a Valley* that was my own introduction to Jean Galbraith; that and the articles that appeared regularly in the *Age*. I was drawn to her down-to-earth approach to the garden and the love of nature that permeated her writing, and I appreciated her sound practical advice.

I first met her in person when she came to my garden at Bleak House. It was very early in my gardening career and I was acutely conscious of her knowledge and gardening wisdom and of my own lack of both. As we walked down a winding path we came upon a little bright pink rose in full flower. Jean asked the name as it was not familiar to her.

'It's just a seedling,' I said. 'I suppose I'll have to move it. It's going to block the path.'

'Well then,' she replied brusquely, 'move the path.'

I have given one of my plants of 'Jean Galbraith' to my dear sister and planted the other four round the base of the three-sided arch in the blacksmith's garden that supports 'Céline Forestier' and 'Claire Jacquier' and the clematis 'Daniel Deronda'. The flowers of 'Jean Galbraith' are a gentle yellow, sometimes faintly flushed with the apricot of its parent. It grew amazingly even in its first year and the bushes are now close to 2 metres high and constantly covered in blooms. I have planted thirty bulbs of the iris 'Professor Blaauw' under them and a new sky-blue geranium, *G. sylvaticum* 'Amy Doncaster'. Poppies are allowed to seed here, and lupins, and of course muscari and the English bluebells I used to cherish and replant whenever I dug them up by mistake until I realised that they are indestructible and will flourish and multiply whatever I do or don't do. I think Jean would have approved of this garden's informality as her own was a country garden.

Despite her extensive knowledge of plants and of botany, hers was not a sophisticated garden. It was devoted to everyday plants – to roses and poppies, delphiniums and marigolds, daisies and foxgloves. She was more concerned with the beauty of the plants she grew than with their rarity. *Garden in a Valley* came out at the beginning of World War II and Jean, whose whole life had been dedicated to gardens and plants, wrote that 'since the thoughts of the world have been concentrated more on things of war than things of peace the peaceful things have become sacred'.

The Jolly Farmer

THE KITCHEN WAS one of the first things we tackled in the house. After all we had to eat. We demolished the hideous makeshift fibro pantry. Behind the fibro we found a door, firmly blocked off, which had given access to what we called the dairy but may have been a creamery or a meat house. There were great black iron hooks attached to the beams in the ceiling – for hanging meat perhaps? Or herbs? And the stone floor sloped down to a grate over a drain. The only window – tall and narrow – was almost obscured by the rose in the courtyard – that enchanting, prickly, early-flowering 'Fortune's Double Yellow'.

We had the door unblocked, put in a new floor and turned this strange little room into a walk-in pantry. The whole kitchen needed a new floor. We used Tasmanian oak, both for the floor and the cupboards. We painted the rough stone walls white and left the heavy beams and the crooked lintels over the doors black, hung my collection of old copper pans and jugs from the beams, installed a new gas stove in the fireplace recess and left it at that.

What I needed now was an old (preferably oak) refectory table and a large (preferably oak) dresser to hold a collection of blue and white china. Despite the steady depredations

Opposite A clump of *Iris pseudacorus* is given the damp conditions it prefers by being near the gently overflowing bowl for the dogs, in the back garden of the Jolly Farmer.

of mainland tourists Tasmania still has a surprising number of antique shops, although many of them stock little in the way of genuine antiques. But in Longford, twenty minutes' drive from Launceston, I found Longford Antiques. The proprietor, Michael McWilliams, specialises in early colonial furniture, for which he has a great love.

Here I found my table – oak, long and narrow, and in its original condition. Michael had four chairs – early Windsor chairs – that could be excellent companions for it. But they were at his home. Perhaps I would care to come over and see them? Of course I would. And I found much more than chairs. I found the most enchanting cottage, furnished entirely with early colonial furniture, set in a 2-acre garden and inhabited not only by Michael but by four dogs, a turkey, decorative hens, pheasants and a cat.

It is called the Jolly Farmer and was built in 1826 as an inn. It gives the impression that little has changed since those early days of white settlement. It is built of rosy handmade bricks, and at the front only a row of ancient almond trees – spellbinding when they burst into blossom in early spring – separate it from the road. The trees still bear each year a large crop of almonds.

I saw the Jolly Farmer first in the gentle light of an early summer evening when the garden was at its peak. I was greeted at the gate by Ikey, a lusty chocolate-brown curly-coated Airedale. I had met him before in the shop and found him nothing if not friendly. But here he was on his home territory. Perhaps he might not be so welcoming. He was barking vociferously but wagging his tail at the same time. It seemed improbable that he would display the same territorial instincts as our heelers.

I pushed the gate open – rather tentatively – and Ikey bounded away down a leafy path in search of his master. The gravel drive was bordered by a lavender hedge and opposite the gate a glorious dogwood, *Cornus kousa*, was in full flower. Tall spires of purple lupins reached up into its lower branches.

Ikey had successfully located Michael, who appeared on a ride-on mower from behind a grand old almond tree that reached to the roof of the nearby stables and was literally covered by little single pink rambler roses. It was one of those vigorous unidentified ramblers that are found in so many early gardens – possibly a multiflora hybrid. I had taken cuttings from just such a rose at the Stables Restaurant in Carrick, where it was successfully blocking the outside stairs and tumbling down from the roof. All my cuttings had taken, as multifloras almost always do, and it is now clothing the big green water tank we installed at the end of our stables, which provides much of the water for the house.

Apart from the almond trees in front of the Jolly Farmer the entire road frontage is planted, as is often the case in Tasmania, with hawthorn, which makes a dense hedge. This, together with the many trees Michael has put in, guarantees complete privacy. Once inside the garden one would never know that there were neighbours and that one was on the outskirts of a small town.

A towering oak tree casts a dense shade. Hellebores and hostas, and many kinds of euphorbia and pulmonaria revel in these conditions. A fine terracotta chimney pot tucked into the edge of the bed houses a tree peony. Michael has a collection of such pots and uses them to fill temporary gaps in the borders or to provide an unexpected splash of colour where one is needed. Beyond the shade garden a dry-stone wall encloses a kitchen garden that is as decorative as it is useful. Roses and foxgloves grow among the artichokes and broad beans and tall spires of garlic.

And then suddenly one comes upon a henhouse inhabited by aristocratic Silver Laced and Gold Laced Wyandottes – no common or garden chooks these – with among them a remarkably handsome rooster called William. Shade is provided here not by the sort of tree one might expect in such a situation – a eucalypt or a peppercorn perhaps – but by a well-grown gingko. This glorious tree – especially glorious in autumn when its leaves turn a clear butter yellow – is worthy of a prominent place in any garden. Its ancestors date back millions of years and it survives unaltered. It never fails to fill me with wonder. As Hugh Johnson remarks in his *Encyclopaedia of Trees*, 'one feels a certain respect for a creature which has simply declined to evolve'.

I have planted one among the roses at Forest Hall. Its history makes the oaks and elms seem youngsters. It is putting on steady growth – as it is in Michael's hen yard, where it seems not to scorn its humble companions. Beneath it, sleeping happily in the late afternoon sunshine, was Jude, an 11-year-old kelpie cross who has only three legs. Michael adopted her when her previous owners died.

The Jolly Farmer may originally have been concerned chiefly with supplying food and

drink to weary travellers; today it supplies a different kind of suste-
nance. It is in every respect a work of art. I was not surprised to learn
that Michael had trained at art school in Hobart.

His studio opens off a courtyard and here he paints, sometimes
on canvas, more often on wood and frequently on pieces of early colonial furniture. The paintings reflect his love of all living things: he
paints not only trees and landscapes but also his own extensive
menagerie. This includes two golden retrievers as well as Ikey and
Jude. Monty is now 14 and spends most of his time sleeping. Heidi was
adopted when her family moved to New South Wales and were reluctant to take her with them. Then there is the cat, a sleek but decidedly
plebian-looking tabby called Olive who, I suspect, rules the roost in
the manner of cats, and skilfully hidden behind a bank of shrubs
another pen of hens, Golden Spangled and Silver Spangled Hamburgs,
with a rooster named Henry II.

The garden too is the work of an artist. Long cool grassy vistas
that curve tantalisingly out of sight are edged with wide mixed borders
filled not so much with rare and unusual plants as with roses and
perennials and all the cottage plants that are so right for the little
house – lupins and foxgloves, poppies and dianthus, aquilegias
and nepetas, a colourful bed of dianthus, a patch of tall sky-blue delphiniums with sunny yellow phlomis, and sheets of the lovely deep
blue *Penstemon serrulatus*, which I have used extensively in my own
garden. In some areas massed planting has achieved bold effects – the

---

Opposite above Wide mixed borders filled with cottage-garden
plants give the one-time inn, built in 1826, the setting it requires.
Opposite below The huge leaves of *Gunnera manicata* tower over
Iris kaempferi, lupins and acanthus and dominate a side border.

giant-sized leaves of *Gunnera manicata* combined with *Iris kaempferi*; and an outsized clump of the brilliant yellow *I. pseudacorus*.

Inside the atmosphere is similar. Michael's collection of early colonial furniture perfectly fits the tiny rooms with their low ceilings, the steep narrow staircase, the low-slung doors that remind us how short many of the settlers were, and the multi-paned windows, each of them looking out over the garden and bringing its warmth and colour into the house.

I took home four hoop-backed Windsor chairs made of elm wood. They sit now in my kitchen looking very comfortable beside the oak table and remind me daily of the rare peace and beauty and harmony of the Jolly Farmer.

Once a
kitchen garden

IF I NEEDED any more evidence – other than the trees, the thousands of bulbs and the old shrubs I had found – that someone had once gardened here, the layout of the garden was sufficient to convince me. Forest Hall is typical of the gardens of its period – parkland in front, a shrubbery to one side and a kitchen garden behind. There was probably a picking garden also but I found no evidence of it. A concrete path led through the kitchen garden – adjacent to the blacksmith's garden on the south-east side – to the drying area. The only thing there not in keeping was a rotary hoist, which we summarily disposed of. (Much later I was sent a photograph of a rotary hoist totally covered by apricot-gold 'Crépuscule' to make a giant umbrella and I was almost – but not entirely – sorry I had done away with mine.)

The kitchen garden, which had been largely devoted to vegetables, was raised about 30 centimetres above the drive, so the drainage was perfect. At the back were two aged and decrepit peach trees long past bearing. Their trunks were covered with moss and lichen and the foliage was sparse. My first inclination was to remove them. But then I thought of the plum tree in our garden at Erinvale and remembered how, when covered with the vigorous ramblers 'The Edna Walling Rose' and 'Tea Rambler', it had become a real feature of the garden. I decided to try to achieve the same effect with the peach trees. But I used different roses.

I was anxious to plant a number of Alister Clark's roses to see how they would fare in this colder climate. So I planted pale pink 'Jessie Clark' at the foot of one of the peach trees

Determined spires of wild garlic still thrust their way up through irises,
lupins, nepetas, lavender and the lovely Hybrid Musk rose 'Penelope' in
what was once a vegetable garden behind the kitchen.

and soft creamy yellow 'Golden Vision' at the foot of the other. As the trees were close together I thought that eventually the roses would intertwine. And to make for greater harmony I planted the deep violet-purple *Clematis viticella* 'Venosa Violacea' beneath each. I need not have worried about the effect of the Tasmanian climate on Alister Clark's roses. Both of these romped in no time to the top of the trees, and the clematis was carried along with them. 'Jessie Clark', peering down from above, is one of the first roses to flower in spring.

On each side of the gate that leads through to the drying area I planted 'Albertine' because I love it so dearly. I should have learnt from my experience with her at Bleak House, where she totally blocked the entrance to the woodshed. But I didn't. So now she stretches her wickedly thorny arms over the gate and is a source of constant annoyance for eleven months of the year and a source of great joy for the remaining one.

At the back of the kitchen garden on its south-east side, the drive leads through a gateway to the stables – a gateway wide enough to have given access to carriages and carts and ploughs in the old days. On one side of this I planted a passionately dark, almost black, red rose given me by a Victorian rosarian, Ian Huxley. It had been bred by a friend of his, Philip Anderson, who had named it – appropriately – 'Philanderer'. It winds its way through a huge clump of the pure white tissue-paper poppy *Romneya coulteri* and thence into one of the peach trees. It is probably the darkest red in the garden.

The kitchen garden is bigger than the blacksmith's garden, measuring some 20 by 15 metres, so I ran a path through it diagonally to make it easier to work – a path that widens to a circle in the middle, where I placed an attractive iron birdbath. The bird life in the garden is a daily delight, especially the families of blue wrens and the occasional redbreasts.

I think it is a very long time since vegetables were grown here. But some of them still have a firm hold on life. The huge crowns of rhubarb, forests of raspberry canes (very difficult to eradicate), whole colonies of potatoes and the purple heads of wild garlic came back time and time again after I thought I had finally got rid of them. And get rid of them I had to for although potagers are very much 'in' and every self-respecting gardener has one, I couldn't persuade myself that growing vegetables for two people justified the time I would need to give them. It was different in the past when the kitchen garden had to feed a household of perhaps twenty people and supermarkets had not been thought of. The potatoes and the garlic, the rhubarb and the raspberries had to go. It took months.

Finally my efforts were crowned with success and work could start on the new garden, a garden devoted in the main to the pink roses that had been rigidly excluded from the sunny courtyard and the blacksmith's garden. And again they were a mixture – early Tea roses, Chinas, Hybrid Musks and even a few Hybrid Perpetuals, then David Austin's English Roses and modern shrub roses – chosen for their historical importance or simply for their beauty. But the colour had to be right. I wanted a harmonious whole and as always aesthetic considerations came first.

I started with the Hybrid Musks – three each of apricot-pink 'Cornelia', paler pink 'Felicia' and almost white, just flushed pink, 'Penelope', probably my favourite. When looking for these I found a plant of 'Francesca', a Hybrid Musk I had not grown before. It was bred by the Reverend Pemberton, the originator of the whole much-treasured family of Hybrid Musks. Like most of the others, 'Francesca' grows into an attractive arching shrub, but its semi-double, rather lethargic-looking flowers are apricot yellow, so they were wrong for this predominantly pink bed. In the end I found a spot for it in the blacksmith's garden near 'Buff Beauty'.

With the Hybrid Musks I planted the strange old China rose *R. chinensis* 'Mutabilis', which changes in colour from apricot in bud, to pink, then deeper pink and finally to almost red. I wanted to pick up all these colours so added the almost equally strange early Tea rose 'Général Galliéni', which varies from buff to red, and the China rose 'Comtesse du Cayla', whose colour has been described variously as apricot, nasturtium red, coppery orange and various shades in between. I was delighted with the one I had planted in the sunny courtyard so added another one here.

Peter Beales describes 'Mme Caroline Testout', bred in France in 1890, as 'one of the world's favourite roses'. And Graham Thomas recalls that it was the first rose he ever purchased, when he was still a schoolboy. I had not grown it in either of my previous gardens but was determined to find a place for it here – it and its parent, the soft pink early Tea rose 'Mme de Tartas', which was used very extensively in breeding.

'Baronne Henriette de Snoy' was an old friend – grown originally for its exotic name.

The ash trees and the stables form the background for this bed of roses, lupins and bulbs. At the far right the pristine 'Penelope' contrasts with the dense foliage of the ash trees. *Opposite above* David Austin's English Rose 'Immortal Juno' needs a tripod (actually a *four*-legged one) to support her exceptionally heavy blooms. *Opposite below* The Hybrid Perpetual 'Reine des Violettes' adds depth of colour to a bed that is predominantly pink.

I had had no great success with it but now I read a description by the American rosarian Brent Dickerson, who described it in *The Old Rose Advisor* as being 'distressing at its worst, beautiful at its best'. He added that 'trial is merited'. I had given it a trial at Bleak House but not a very fair one. It had been grown in a badly drained bed and had suffered all the winter with wet feet. One of its parents was the temperamental 'Gloire de Dijon' so it could hardly be expected to tolerate such conditions. I decided to give it another, fairer trial and planted it next to 'Comtesse du Cayla', with whom its peach-pink flowers blended beautifully.

'Sally Holmes' was bred in the UK as recently as 1976. It bears single creamy white flowers that open from an apricot bud. They are borne in such large and spectacular clusters that one alone would make a bouquet fit for a bride. I had seen it in Heather Cant's garden near Bowral and resolved then and there that if I ever made another garden I would plant 'Sally Holmes'. It needs space for it forms a large shrub and is best, like so many things, grown in a group of three or four together. In fact I would love to grow this rose as a hedge. I have contented myself with two plants and they have done splendidly. Behind them I put two plants of the rather leggy, undisciplined Hybrid Musk rose 'Vanity'. Perhaps because of its vivid lipstick-pink colour this lovely single rose is not planted often enough. But with 'Sally Holmes' as a foil and violet-blue, late-flowering irises at its feet it is a joy.

Equally spaced along the path that cuts diagonally through this garden I erected three very pretty tripods – dark green with domed heads. On the first I planted the David Austin rose 'Immortal Juno'. It was difficult to find as apparently David Austin has stopped distributing it because it does not stand up to wet weather. That may be so in England but in Tasmania I find it one of the most rewarding of the David Austin roses. In shape and in scent it resembles an old rose and its colour is superb – warm pink shot through with lilac. The bush is big and inclined to be straggly, hence the tripod. It reached the top in one season and the large, heavy blooms spill over.

On the second tripod I had meant to plant the Bourbon rose 'Mme Ernst Calvat'. It arrived in July bare rooted and I planted it in good faith expecting warm pink blooms to blend with those of 'Immortal Juno'. I lost interest in it for a while as it seemed disinclined to flower, and when it finally burst into bloom and drew attention to itself I was surprised (and disappointed) to find that instead of 'Mme Ernst Calvat' I appeared to have the white

Hybrid Musk 'Pax'. It's a fine rose and I would have been quite happy to give it garden room, but somewhere else – say, with the single, bright pink 'Vanity'. It did nothing for 'Immortal Juno'.

For the third tripod I chose the delightful silvery pink Hybrid Perpetual 'Mrs John Laing'. The nearly thornless bush will reach well over 1.5 metres so is eminently suitable for growing as a pillar rose. 'Mrs John Laing' has a host of admirers, not least among them Dean Hole himself, the eminent nineteenth-century rosarian, who described her as being 'not only in vigour, constancy and abundance but in form and feature Beauty's Queen'. She was bred in the UK in 1887 and has been beloved by generations of gardeners ever since.

I found a prominent spot for 'Heritage', one of the loveliest of David Austin's roses – glowing pink, double and quartered, deliciously scented and almost thornless. I could never leave her out.

All these pinks needed a touch of darker colour so I added three more all-time favourites – the deep violet-purple Hybrid Perpetual 'Reine des Violettes', the even darker, tall-growing Moss rose 'William Lobb' and the intriguing 'Tour de Malakoff' – pink, purple and violet blended, and named according to Brent Dickerson for the role the tower of Malakoff played in the defence of Sebastopol in the Crimean War.

Less exotic – in fact very far from exotic – is the Australian-bred 'Midnight Sun'. The description was enticing – darkest red verging on black – but the bush turned out to be spindly (my fault perhaps) and the flowers, although the dark red I had been led to expect, were not remarkable. I think sentence has been passed on it and next winter may see it consigned to the scrap heap and replaced by something better able to live up to the performance of its aristocratic neighbours. 'Général Jacqueminot' perhaps? Its brilliant red colouring caused it to be used extensively in breeding. It numbers among its offspring such

---

Following pages left The heavily scented blooms of David Austin's 'Heritage' resemble the flowers of an old cabbage rose, but unlike those they are borne for months on end. *Following pages right* The stems and buds of 'William Lobb' are heavily mossed. This Moss rose grows tall, and its branches reach up into a nearby peach tree.

famous roses as 'Souvenir du Docteur Jamain'. 'Général Jacqueminot' was bred in France in 1853 by Auguste Roussel, who bred roses as a hobby. To his great disappointment he never really succeeded in breeding a first-class rose. The day after he died his gardener found 'Général Jacqueminot' among his very last lot of seedlings.

The general for whom this grand old Hybrid Perpetual was named was one of Napoleon's officers. Among his other achievements he is credited with establishing a brewery in Paris. But fame is fleeting. Ethel Turner wrote of the general in her book *The Ungardeners*:

Who is there now knows aught of his story?
What is left of him but a name?
Of him who shared in Napoleon's glory
And dreamed that his sword had won him fame?
Oh, the fate of a man is past discerning!
Little did Jacqueminot suppose
At Austerlitz or at Moscow's burning
That his fame would rest in the heart of a rose.

A worthier companion perhaps for 'Tour de Malakoff'? I added two more Australian-bred roses to the General's bed – both pink – that I find entrancing. Alister Clark's 'Sheila Bellair' is one of my favourites among Clark's roses – a glowing pink and semi-single. George Thomson's 'Mrs Mary Thomson' bears semi-double mauve-pink flowers with marked golden stamens and a tantalising perfume. It is the result of a cross between David Austin's charming, rustic-looking 'Dapple Dawn' and the ever-popular 'Ophelia'.

At the back of the tall, wide bed on the far side hollyhocks reach up into the peach trees. Prostrate rosemary trails over a retaining wall. Masses of deep red herbaceous peonies – a legacy from an earlier gardener – are a feature of the spring. Lupins – mauve and white, pink and carmine – lilac-blue *Iris xiphium* and pink tritonias are firmly established. Pale green nicotianas are planted each year to fill the gaps and tall bearded irises line the paths. Every now and again I still find a potato pushing its way through and a mauve drumstick head of wild garlic peeping out among the roses.

The shrubbery

APART FROM THE venerable trees, the oldest part of the garden was the shrubbery. For many months I skirted round it. It was impossible to do anything else. It was a jungle of overgrown trees and unpruned shrubs carpeted by lamium and vinca and ivy, a trap for unwary feet, and blackberry that trailed down from the trees and grabbed one's hair and one's clothes and rendered the whole thing impenetrable.

By our first spring at Forest Hall I had decided that the shrubbery could be ignored no longer. It was the ancient *Magnolia grandiflora* nearby that spurred me into action. It produced half a dozen of its languid, heavily scented, ivory flowers and gave promise of better things to come if only it could be given the occasional drink of water and be freed from the blackberry that was threatening to choke it.

I started on the side nearest the house where there was a huge amorphous mass of variegated ivy. Two days of cutting and pulling revealed the stone chimney of an old bread oven. The ivy had not only spread beyond the shrubbery to cover the chimney, but had extended rapacious arms along the kitchen wall and right up to the eaves, and along the wall of the barn opposite, clinging tenaciously to the stone.

At the foot of the magnolia was a thicket of *Philadelphus coronarius* – the mock orange beloved by all Victorian gardeners. There had been one in the garden of my childhood and my mother had loved it and brought in great sprays for the house. It was many a long year since this old chap had had any attention, but he put on a brave show for us in

The shrubbery makes a dramatic
backdrop to a circular bed on the
lawn beyond. The circle is edged
with a hedge of *Lonicera nitida*
and has as its centrepiece a
standardised *Escallonia* 'Apple
Blossom'. Under the crab apples
in the bed on the left are the
gallicas that now give this part
of the garden its name – the
cardinals' walk.

this, our first spring. And on the south-west side of the barn the biggest Chinese snowball tree I had ever seen covered itself with round white balls that I could pick from the first-storey windows. The shrubbery was my own miniature Heligan – untold treasures might lie hidden here.

A week's labour saw two rusted barbed-wire fences removed and a mountain of black-berry and ivy and lamium and vinca carted up the paddock to be burnt. At the end of a fort-night we could penetrate right to the heart of the shrubbery.

A white japonica, *Chaenomeles speciosa* 'Nivalis', was home to several families of little blue wrens, who must have deeply resented our intrusion into their sanctuary. Entwined in its branches – and in the branches of almost all the shrubs – was that most tenacious of all weeds, sticky Willy, known to the locals by the less colourful name of cleavers. It stuck to our hands and our clothes and the coats of the dogs.

Deep blue ceanothus were here. But ceanothus are not long lived and our two were so old and sad and neglected that, reluctantly, I took them out and resolved to plant another. I did, much later – the prostrate powder-blue *C. gloriosus* 'Emily Brown' I found at Woodbank Nursery, near Hobart, and planted among the yellow roses in front of the black-smith's cottage.

There was a choisya too, and a multitude of lilacs, mauve and white and deep purple – not sophisticated 'improved' varieties but the common, heavily scented lilacs of our child-hood. And a weeping forsythia, *F. suspensa*, a fountain of gold in earliest spring.

Right at the centre was a giant cordyline – it seems that no nineteenth-century gar-den was complete without one. This one was a monster and at its feet was a deep, wide burrow discovered early in the piece by Joh, one of our heelers, who dug frantically until more than half of his body had disappeared down the hole. But despite his best endeavours – and he returned to it day after day – we never did discover who owned the burrow. It was too big for rabbits. I suspect it belonged to a wombat. It was big enough for that and we had seen many of them in the paddocks.

I wanted the cordyline out. I can see nothing beautiful in their stiff, unyielding lines. But I thought the task beyond me. I mentioned it conversationally one afternoon to John and within half an hour it was gone, leaving nothing but Joh's excavation and a clear view down to the waters of the lake. I think the wombat must have sought another home at this juncture for we saw no further evidence of him and Joh's frantic digging came to an end.

The dominant feature of the shrubbery was a fine variegated holly. Just after Christmas we had a visit from some Victorian people who had lived here many years ago. With them was an elderly aunt – in her late eighties perhaps – who had happy childhood memories of Forest Hall. It was the holly that delighted her most.

'It's Great-aunt Mary's holly!' she cried. 'She grew it from seed and planted it there.'

Old records found by another member of the family confirmed that it had indeed been planted by Mary Bonnily in 1870. So we have cherished and nourished it and it is still known as Great-aunt Mary's holly. It is strongly variegated and one small branch right at the base of the tree in deepest shade is entirely cream with no sign of green, no trace of chlorophyll.

Perhaps Great-aunt Mary also planted the sorbus, *S. hupehensis* from China, with its deep blue-green foliage and white berries tinted a delicate shade of pink. Like the holly, it sets masses of seed and little seedlings are found throughout the garden. It reminded me of the many sorbus we had grown in Victoria, and later I planted in the daffodil paddock *S. domestica* and the very lovely *S. aria* 'Lutescens' with its silver-grey foliage.

Two large unruly bushes of *Lonicera nitida* and one of *Teucrium fruticans* needed drastic treatment. Both make excellent hedges so I took dozens of cuttings and kept them in reserve for use later.

Tucked in tightly against the stone wall of the barn, hidden by a dense curtain of ivy and wisteria, I uncovered an old outdoor toilet – a two seater. We demolished it without regrets and in its place I planted two camellias, which we espaliered along the wall – tiny white species camellias with narrow foliage that is attractive in its own right.

There were sheets of Japanese windflowers (*Anemone hupehensis*), both white and mauve, and masses of honesty (*Lunaria annua*), again both white and mauve, which had seeded all through the shrubbery. And – not so welcome – in early summer hundreds of the harsh yellow and orange alstroemeria, the so-called Peruvian lily. There were none of the lovely subtle colours developed later in the ligtu hybrids. I remembered the orange ones growing like this in old gardens at the top of Mt Macedon where all attempts to

eradicate them had proved ineffectual. Months later I found, up in the paddocks bordering the small plantation of nashi fruit, hundreds of alstroemerias that had obviously been planted there. Had some previous owner had visions of growing them as a cash crop, I wondered.

I started to remove the ones in the shrubbery forthwith but they still come back each summer. The yellow ones are tolerable among the banks of blue hydrangeas but I cannot persuade myself to like the orange ones. Nor the orange montbretias that, resisting all my onslaughts, emerge again triumphantly every spring.

Despite the weeks of back-breaking work involved in reducing the shrubbery to some sort of manageable order, I loved it from the outset. This had been no casual country garden thrown together from bits and pieces gleaned from neighbours. Knowledgeable and loving hands had been at work here. Like the trees, it was a legacy from the past and it was my responsibility to hand it on. And apart from anything else it was the only really shady area in the garden, one of the few places in which I could plant true shade-loving plants.

Once the rubbish had been removed I was left not only with plenty of shade but with one large central area in filtered sunlight. Here I planted my favourite viburnum, *V. plicatum* 'Mariesii', which bears its umbels of white flowers on horizontal, outstretched branches. I remembered seeing it first in the garden of that famous English gardener Margery Fish, at East Lambrook Manor in Somerset. I had fallen in love with it there. In fact I had fallen in love with the whole garden, not much more than an acre but every corner and cranny carefully and lovingly tended. When I got back to Australia I sought out her books and returned to them again and again – especially the first one, *We Made a Garden* – where I found both information and inspiration. This viburnum serves as a reminder of the very happy day I spent there. With it I planted the lovely *Carpentaria californica* to which I was first introduced by another great gardener, Joan Law-Smith, at Bolobek. It is evergreen

Opposite In the shrubbery under Great-aunt Mary's holly, the sorbus and the viburnum – in fact wherever I could find a spare corner – I planted hellebores as ground cover, in all shades from white through to deepest claret.

and its small, single white flowers are not unlike those of a philadelphus – the essence of purity and simplicity.

Paths were essential. We made three with white gravel, which wind their way through the shrubbery and emerge near a circular bed in the lawn on the south-east side. I surrounded this bed with a hedge made from the lonicera cuttings. They grow fast – almost too fast as they need frequent clipping. The centrepiece of the bed is a standardised *Escallonia* 'Apple Blossom'. Underneath it I put my favourite piece of sculpture, which I have had in my garden since my days at Bleak House – a slender little madonna, the work of the Bavarian sculptor Hans Knorr. Round her feet in spring is a mass of the low-growing, late-flowering, double pink tulip 'Angélique'.

Under a tall, vase-shaped cotoneaster growing in the poor, dry soil of the shrubbery, I found a patch of *Cyclamen hederifolium* struggling beneath the blanket of ivy and vinca, yet still flowering bravely. (Later I was given dozens from the rich supply at Beulah and Dunedin, two of Tasmania's truly great gardens.) Also hellebores, not in ones and twos but by the dozen. And hostas, and the lovely pulmonarias, with their leaves spotted white and their flowers pink and heavenly blue.

The following spring, at the end of an unusually long, cold winter – leaden skies and sleety rain that confined us to the house for weeks – we decided to visit the garden of John Mott, renowned for its primroses. The day was perfect and the road ran along by the sea until we turned inland at Ulverstone. And when we got there the primroses were in flower. Not in their hundreds, but in their thousands. They carpeted the ground under the trees and shrubs, lined all the paths and filled us with intense excitement. It was a day to remember. Carried away by the spirit of spring we bought boxes of them. As we left, John Mott presented each of us with a very special double white one.

I was reminded of a book I had picked up in an antiquarian bookshop. The opening sentence was obviously written by a Londoner who had had an even more trying winter than ours: 'Once I remember well, when I was hungering for a breath of country air, a woman, brown with the caresses of wind and sun, brought the spring to my door and sold it to me for a penny.' It was of primroses that she wrote. I planted mine in the shrubbery along the edges of the paths, with *Alchemilla mollis* that I had found under the mulberry tree.

In this part of the garden perhaps more than anywhere else I was and still am constantly reminded of those who have gardened here before me, who have loved and cherished this house and its surroundings and left their mark upon it. I kept coming across new treasures. In the second spring masses of Solomon's seal pushed through and a tiny patch of *Fritillaria meleagris*.

But it was another year before I found, under a bank of the little red *Fuchsia magellanica* intertwined with a huge mass of the pale pink rose 'Bloomfield Abundance', a flight of stone steps ascending from the shrubbery to the lawn in front of the house.

A double white hellebore

AMONG THE HELLEBORES in the shrubbery is a very special one. It is a rare double white and was named 'Betty Ranicar' as a tribute to a very special gardener. Betty's garden, Red Hill, lies not far from Deloraine on the road that runs through to Mole Creek. The dignified old house, originally a coaching inn, is set right on the road and if you drive slowly and look carefully you may catch a glimpse, through the hedge, of a gem of a garden. It is not big. Perhaps an acre. But everything in it has been chosen with discernment and tended with loving care.

When Betty moved to Red Hill from India as a young wife, with three small sons, there was no garden. And the needs of the farm came first. Over the years from a bare paddock Betty created what has come to be recognised as one of the loveliest small gardens in Australia.

Gradually the garden assumed more and more importance in her life and came to fill many of her waking hours. Fortunately for us she started to keep a garden diary. Not only did she record her activities day by day and month by month, but she made sketches in precise detail of many of the plants that meant most to her, with accompanying descriptions.

Opposite This double white hellebore, now much sought after, was named for a very gifted Tasmanian gardener – Betty Ranicar of Red Hill.

The diaries listed the flowering times of many plants. The garden was 'probably at its peak third week in November', and the list of plants flowering then gives some idea of how densely planted this garden was.

It was in summer that I usually visited the garden, long before we settled at Forest Hall – visits that coincided with our fishing trips to Tasmania. But whatever time of year you came to Red Hill, the garden was glorious. Betty recorded the fact that it was usually in December that she started watering: 'lawn browning – the bloom has gone'. However, in February when many gardens are looking tired and drooping, the list of things flowering was as long as ever. And in April, with autumn and cold weather fast approaching, she was continuing to list roses, sweet peas, nerines, cyclamen and many more. Even in the last week of May she still recorded a few roses: '"Titian" and floribundas for the house, violets, jasmine and fuchsias.' In June it was 'sasanqua camellias, ericas, hellebores, bergenia, winter jasmine'. July brought the first of the snowflakes, crocuses and primroses. By August the names filled a whole page and chionodoxas and erythroniums had joined the evergrowing list of bulbs.

There was much practical advice in the diaries: 'Prune Connie Spry to three feet after flowering, Rosa Mundi to two.' I would not have the courage to do that but hers were the best plants of 'Rosa Mundi' I have seen so obviously her technique was appreciated.

There was more advice to rose growers: 'Feed roses fish manure as buds form.' And in December: 'Gave roses each a tablespoon of Epsom Salts.'

She was ruthless about getting rid of those plants that failed to perform: 'List of roses to discard – Michelle Meilland, Grandmere Jenny, Anne Letts.'

Betty grew most of her own vegetables and the diaries included useful tips such as 'To ripen green tomatoes put above the dozen into a sealed plastic bag with two or three ripe apples.'

She recorded the presence of creatures that lived in the garden. She wrote often 'trouble with rabbits', and in February 1963 'Kookaburra ate my goldfish.' On 7 May 1963 'rabbits eaten a whole row of carrots', and the following month 'O'Meara's pig spent several hours last night in the vegetable garden – parsnips, turnips and spinach eaten.' In August 'The first daffodils out and the first blackbird sang.' In November, as the weather got warmer, 'I nearly put my hand on a snake below the wall.' And in January 'Honeyeater family – parents and four children – bathed in the birdbath. Blackbirds still singing.'

Frequently noted in the diaries was 'Blanch came.' Betty made frequent lists for Blanch, which included jobs such as pruning the fruit trees and the roses, weeding the raspberries and cleaning paths. She ticked them off as they were done.

I had only ever known one Blanch. A close friend of my mother. Tall and elegant. Her house as elegant as herself, and furnished with Georgian treasures. As a child I stood in awe of her. As an adolescent I respected and revered her. As a young adult I visited her whenever I came back to my home town, spent hours in the garden with her and was introduced to the poetry of Gerard Manley Hopkins and the *Stundenbuch* of the German mystic Rainer Maria Rilke, which she read in the original and translated for me. I think the garden had a mystical element for her. We live in an age that has lost its sense of wonder, an age that refers to an athlete's performance or a company's profit as 'awesome', but she had seen the miracle of plants bursting into flower, of bulbs pushing up through bare brown earth, of seed germinating. These memories came flooding back each time I read in Betty's diaries that 'Blanch came.'

In the winter of 1962 Betty made a pool. On 4 June she 'collected stones below the road for my pool'. And then on 6 June 'Blanch excavated the pool. I went to Deloraine and purchased the polythene to line same.' For the first time it occurred to me that this invaluable Blanch, who seemed to have so many skills and such physical strength, might be a man, not the staunch woman friend I had taken her to be. And this turned out to be the case, Blanch being his surname. He was a jobbing gardener with no suggestion of elegance and decidedly no element of mysticism about him.

Together Blanch and Betty finally finished the pool. On 15 June Betty recorded that she 'spent some hours on the pool placing flat rocks round the edge'. And on 5 July 'I finished off the pool this afternoon.' But this was not the end of the story. In August she wrote: 'Lots of trouble with the pool. It began to leak badly and had to be concreted.'

The pool became in the end one of the outstanding features of the garden. Round it she planted some of the many bulbs she grew from seed – crocuses, fritillarias and cyclamen that multiplied as the years went by. By the time of my first visit to Red Hill they had formed a dense tapestry.

Hostas, pulmonarias and
campanulas carpet the shady
beds in the long-established
garden that was Betty Ranicar's.
Opposite above A red rose at
Red Hill. Its name – if it ever
had one – was never recorded.
Opposite below Lupins,
Cerastium tomentosum and
delphiniums fill the sunny
bank above a dry-stone
wall at Red Hill.

There was rarely a day when Betty did not list some garden activity in her diary – unless she was away fishing. She was a skilled angler and spent long summer days fishing in tranquil, tree-lined Penstock Lagoon in the Central Highlands. Inclement weather never deterred her. On 11 June 1962 she noted 'Bitterly cold – fog all day', but on that same day she was out planting and the next day went to Perth to order trees. On 3 July 1962 she wrote 'Very cold and snow showers – bought white delphiniums and white Japanese iris and rose "White Bouquet".' And in August she recorded a trip to Hobart: 'Terribly cold, snow in south and frosts here. Put in some new plants . . .'

The double white hellebore has become popular with discerning gardeners and is widely sought after. This year mine has seeded I think, and I should be able to move the tiny seedlings in the gravel path into a bed of their own so that next year I should have quite a dense planting – a permanent reminder of one of the greatest gardeners I have known.

The cardinals' walk

ON THE SOUTH-EAST SIDE of the garden at Forest Hall, beyond the shrubbery, the lawn stretches away towards the daffodil paddock and the lake. Here I had made the little circular bed surrounded by a low hedge enclosing the standardised *Escallonia* 'Apple Blossom' and the slender madonna. But the bed looked lonely out there by itself.

The land slopes gently from here up to the high convict-built stone wall in front of the stables, where under three ancient ash trees whose drooping branches reach almost to the ground we had put a table and chairs. This had become a favourite place for lunch on hot summer days or drinks on cool autumn evenings. The spot was marred only by the fact that from where we sat the view was interrupted by the Bass Highway. What was needed was a barrier of shrubs that would grow tall enough to blot out the highway but not so tall as to interfere with the glorious view of mountains beyond.

Following pages left The shade cast by a group of three ancient ash trees, some of whose branches reach almost to the ground, has made the lawn in front of the stables a favourite sitting place. *Following pages right* The vibrant pink gallica rose 'Complicata' is one of several old-fashioned shrub roses in the first of the two beds I planted to border this lawn.

In the end I designed two long parallel borders beyond the circular bed and curving gently towards the daffodil paddock. I started initially with one – the top one, nearer to the ash trees. It is planted with the striking viburnum known as 'Notcutt's Variety', which covers itself with brilliant scarlet berries rather like red currants; *Magnolia* 'Star Wars'; an unknown pink sasanqua camellia; and a dear little, delightfully scented, white-flowered bush that was a gift to the garden and whose name completely escapes me.

To these I added roses – tall-growing shrub roses that would attain a height of at least 2 metres. As is my habit, wherever possible I planted three of each. First choice was R. × *alba* 'Maxima', both for its beauty and its historical connections. It is known variously as Bonnie Prince Charlie's Rose, the Jacobite Rose and the White Rose of York, and it has graced English gardens since the fifteenth century. Added to this it is hardy and long lived and has a delicious perfume. Then came 'Frühlingsmorgen', a spinosissima hybrid nearly as lovely as 'Frühlingsgold'; R. *willmottiae*, for no better reason than that I had a few plants left over; 'Fantin Latour', which was given a place of honour near a little wooden gate that leads into a grassy patch above the daffodil paddock (one day I shall plant a hedge of 'Fantin Latour'); and 'Complicata', the lovely 'Complicata', with its large single blooms of a radiant pink such as is seldom found among old roses. I hoped it might climb into the lower branches of the nearer of two walnut trees – Graham Thomas has a 'Complicata' in his garden that he says has grown 3 metres into an apple tree. He believes it 'should be in every garden where shrubs are grown'. These are all once-flowering roses so I put in three of the Bourbon rose 'Honorine de Brabant'. Pale pink striped deeper pink and mauve, it has one good flowering and then continues intermittently throughout the season.

Along the front of the bed I planted clumps of pink and deep blue and palest yellow *Iris innominata*, which need almost no attention. I shall divide them up next winter.

This border established itself quite quickly but the little round bed with the escallonia was still sitting in splendid isolation in the middle of the lower lawn. So I got to work on a second border parallel to the first. It was designed to be taller so that from the ash trees one could look across the roses of the first border to this second one.

It is planted principally with trees belonging to the Rosaceae family. First the crab apples – *Malus floribunda*, *M. toringoides* and 'Golden Hornet', with its delectable golden apples; next two medlars with white flowers that could pass for those of a species rose, and fruit that I am told is edible but have never been able to bring myself to try; then the tansy-leaved thorn *Crataegus tanacetifolia*, which has strange, almost dark grey foliage and small yellow fruits that resemble rose hips; and lastly one of my favourite small trees (which, however, does not belong to the rose family), the Japanese snowbell, *Styrax japonicus*.

This brought us down to the *Magnolia grandiflora* to the south-east of the shrubbery. I was inclined to leave it at that. Then at the end of August came a large parcel from Nieuwesteeg's Rose Nursery. Bill brought it home from the post office in some puzzlement.

'You've already had John's roses for this year,' he said, 'so what's this?'

I was as mystified as he was. But any rose parcel is a good parcel. I opened it forthwith. Inside I found a note from John. 'I know you probably don't want sixteen cardinals in the garden. But the alternative is the bonfire,' he wrote. And I unwrapped sixteen splendid 2-year-old plants of the old gallica rose 'Cardinal de Richelieu'. It is one of my (many) favourites. Its dark velvety purple colouring, the colour of a cardinal's robes, is a wonderful addition to the rose gardener's predominantly pink and white palette. I was delighted.

The only problem lay in deciding where to plant them. But it was obvious really. Sixteen plants just over a metre apart would fit comfortably in front of the crab apples. So we widened the bed and christened this section of the garden the cardinals' walk.

The following year I experimented with various underplantings – smoky pink *Sedum* 'Vera Jameson'; several different campanulas; pale pink cranesbills. But the blues carried the day. They were stunning against the purple roses. I made a generous planting of the lilac-blue *Penstemon serrulatus* and the slightly paler blue 'Sensation', with the strange, almost navy-blue cerinthe and blue campanulas.

Between the cardinals' walk and its top border the ground slopes gently upwards. One day I was standing looking across the lawn to the high stone wall behind the ash trees while John was putting stones in place to form an edging.

'What we really need of course,' I said reflectively, 'is a low stone retaining wall below the first border.'

'I could build that,' John said quietly.

I pointed out the difficulties inherent in dry-stone walling. But he was undeterred.

The roses in the first border include 'Fantin Latour', 'Honorine de Brabant' and *R. × alba* 'Semi-plena' as well as 'Complicata'. Under the branches of the nearby walnut tree one glimpses the lake.

Bill had invested in a sturdy four-wheeled motorbike for use in the garden. It pulled an equally sturdy red trailer and was the joy of my life. It carried grass clippings, prunings, weeds, sand, gravel, pea straw; it carried my tools from one part of the garden to the next. That very afternoon John took it out into the paddock and started collecting flat stones. Over the next few days he worked steadily and meticulously. His arms and shoulders are immensely strong. One by one he lifted the heavy stones into place. By the end of the following week the wall was completed. It is a work of art, fitted together skilfully like the pieces of a puzzle.

And John loved it. Building the wall provided an outlet for his strong creative instincts. Since that day he has constructed no fewer than five stone walls in the garden. And an alcove for a stone seat. And a flight of wide stone steps. As the early dry-stone walls speak of the convicts who built them and left their mark on this place, so these speak of John and his own long-lasting contribution.

The upper lawn was now bordered to the north-east and south-west by stone walls. We curved the border above John's first wall right round the south-east side of the lawn. This left only the north-west side undefined. Here the lawn meets the drive as it winds round to the stables, and I decided to plant a rose hedge. Not too tall. From our position under the ash trees I wanted to be able to look across it to the barn and the house.

I must have chosen – and subsequently rejected – at least a dozen roses before a decision was made. 'Fantin Latour'? Too tall. *R. centifolia*? Too unruly. Rugosas? Too dense and thick. 'Sally Holmes'? Not compact enough. 'Stanwell Perpetual'? I had grown a very successful hedge of that at Bleak House. Finally I settled on the little Hybrid Musk rose 'Ballerina'. It is almost constantly in flower – simple single pink flowers, with a white eye, borne in huge panicles. It has few thorns. It doesn't grow too tall. Bred in 1937 it was put out by John Bentall, who had worked with the Reverend Pemberton right up until his death and had seen the development of that marvellous family of Hybrid Musks – 'Penelope', 'Cornelia', 'Felicia'. Recent research seems to indicate that it was in fact John Bentall's wife, Ann, who was responsible for 'Ballerina', but after the fashion of good wives of that era she allowed her husband to take full credit.

It was necessary to leave a break in the hedge to give access from the lawn to the drive. So we made the break a wide and generous one and I had a gifted local man make me a high double archway of green metal. On this I planted yet another of my favourites, the glorious, fruity scented, recurrent-flowering, lemony white Noisette rose 'Lamarque'.

Bridget Gubbins, who holds the clematis collection for the Australian Ornamental Plant Conservation Association, has published a delightful and very informative little book called *Growing Clematis*. She told me once that it is quite feasible to plant a rose and a clematis in the one hole. So I tried it. I planted 'Lamarque' with *C. viticella* 'Alba Luxurians', which produces a rather ragged, milk-white bloom, the petals tipped with green. It has been a great success. Both rose and clematis seem happy and I give the clematis a hard prune in winter.

In the middle of the upper lawn I then constructed a large circular bed in which we placed an obelisk. It is a perfectly splendid obelisk, 3 metres tall, made of timber painted the same forest green as the arch, and designed and fashioned by Ray Joyce. Ray is an artist as well as a very fine professional photographer. He and his partner, Elaine Rushbrooke, own the lovely rose garden and nursery in the south of the island called the Scented Rose. They specialise in David Austin's English Roses. I had seen and admired the obelisks Ray had made for this garden and he offered to make one for me.

The central bed was the perfect place for it. Standing on the drive you look through the arch across the lawn to the obelisk and then on to the wooden gate. I edged this bed with a box hedge, which I intend to keep low. On the obelisk itself I planted the thornless, recurrent-flowering, pink climbing rose 'Renae'. And with it the large-flowered, white clematis 'Duchess of Edinburgh'. In the bed I planted three each of the David Austin rose 'Redouté' and the Hybrid Perpetual 'Frau Karl Druschki'. 'Redouté' must be one of David Austin's greatest successes. A sport of the very popular 'Mary Rose', it is the softest, most delicate pink, very double, very recurrent, disease resistant and deliciously scented. I chose 'Frau Karl Druschki' because I wanted to keep this bed to pink and white and she is the whitest rose I know. Not a tinge of pink or cream. Snow white. In fact she was known as the 'Snow Queen' – a cold fairytale character. The name was chosen perhaps because this rose, like snow, has absolutely no scent. But in this situation this doesn't worry me for 'Redouté' has scent enough for both.

The sixteen plants of the purple gallica 'Cardinal de Richelieu' in the second border have given their name to the walk that runs between the two beds. *Opposite above* Three each of David Austin's English Rose 'Redouté' and the Hybrid Perpetual 'Frau Karl Druschki' surround the obelisk that forms the centrepiece of the upper lawn. *Opposite below* The striped Bourbon rose 'Honorine de Brabant' flowers recurrently and provides colour when the blooms of the other roses in the first border are over.

For early spring – before the roses have woken from their dormancy – I planted a hundred bulbs of the late-flowering tulip 'Upstar' – pink of course. This would ensure a splendid display in October, but even late-flowering tulips are over by the time the roses come seriously into bloom. I would need to have something coming on to take their place.

I decided on zinnias, even though they would need to be replanted each year. I used to dislike these tough little annuals with their rather stiff petals, their flowers the colour of posterpaints and their unremarkable foliage. Then, some years ago, I saw in the potager at Cruden Farm in Victoria low-growing, acid-green zinnias planted among the vegetables. It was an arresting sight.

The zinnias come into flower in early summer and continue through to the end of autumn while the tulips are safely underground. And they go by the very appropriate name of 'Envy'.

The walnut tree

IT WAS A STILL, sunny afternoon in late summer. There was not a breath of wind to ruffle the leaves of the old walnuts of the cardinals' walk, underneath which I was working. I had been cutting back the nepeta – with Willy and Joh supervising – and carting it in barrowloads to the compost heap.

Suddenly the stillness was shattered by a sharp report and Willy and Joh took to their heels and ran and I, without thinking, but feeling instinctively that they knew what they were about, followed them.

There was another loud crack, succeeded by a dull thud and the bigger of the two walnuts lay on the ground. Without warning, and for no apparent reason, it had broken off at its base, missing the dogs and me by centimetres.

Standing there, my heart pounding, I wondered inconsequentially whether dogs were subject to the same adrenaline rush as humans in situations such as this. But there they were, sitting nonchalantly on the lawn as though nothing had happened, unaware apparently that they had just had a near brush with death, while I was shaking like the proverbial aspen leaf.

The tree had done remarkably little damage to the garden, although it had fallen across John's so recently constructed dry-stone wall, demolishing it utterly, and it had broken several branches of the old mulberry tree nearby.

But it is difficult to accept such a sudden and radical change. Its absence left a great hole in the landscape and exposed much of that part of the garden to the view of passing

The grand walnut near the cardinals' walk is the companion of the one
underneath which the dogs and I were working on the day of its demise.
The loss gave us a wider view of the landscape beyond.

traffic on the Bass Highway, which we had been so intent on blocking out. This was to be deplored, but on the other hand it had exposed considerably more of the wonderful line of mountains that make up the Western Tiers.

It is strange how much bigger a tree looks lying on the ground than it does when erect. Now prostrate, the walnut covered most of that section of lawn and looked immense.

Walnuts are not fast growing. We would not be able to replace it in a lifetime.

The first priority was to find someone to remove it, since it was a task beyond our limited practical abilities. In the first place it needed a powerful chainsaw and a large truck.

I looked at its lush green foliage and its rough, ghostly grey fissured bark and felt a rush of pity for the old fellow. Had the bees nesting in his trunk been partly responsible, I wondered. Or was it simply a case of advancing years? His companion on the other side of the lawn had almost certainly been planted at the same time – by William Bonnily himself, no doubt – and it looked to be in fine fettle. But so had this one until a few minutes ago.

And what was to be done with the timber?

Walnut is prized. It is such very beautiful timber both in colour and grain. To burn it would be sacrilege. So I visited the local gallery and inquired who made the variety of sculptures often on display there. The proprietor gave me a number of names. These sculptors, she assured me, all worked in wood and could well be interested in the walnut. I went home and made some calls. Several expressed interest.

The next morning John came and started patiently to rebuild the wall, a wall into whose construction he had put so much care. The stones were sorted and laid aside for use later. At least we did not have to search for any more. He was sitting on his customary seat – a discarded milk crate – putting in the bottom layer of stones when the first of the sculptors arrived.

The moment he opened his mouth I knew he was not the man for us. He was not strong, he said. He lived on the pension. He was not well off like some people. He could not afford to pay for the tree. (I had not mentioned money – finding a home for the walnut was almost as personal a thing as finding a home for the puppies Willy had sired.) It was a big job, he said. It would all have to be carted away, and really he wasn't sure he would have a use for so much timber.

I glanced down at John, sitting there patiently lifting heavy stone after heavy stone and fitting them into position.

John said nothing. He didn't even look up.

But his face was expressive. In the two years he had been coming to us I had never heard him complain, never heard him mention his disability.

So I packed him off, this ailing sculptor, telling him it was apparent the job was not for him.

Half an hour later Paul Nordanus arrived. Young and strong, cheerful and confident, a craftsman to his very bootstraps. He said little but stood looking down on the splendid old tree, and I felt that he was, like the sculptor Hans Knorr, 'seeing the glory where the sap once rose, the thick trunk soared, the branch broke forth'.

'What a beauty,' he said finally. 'I would love it. I can't pay you what it's worth. But I could give you one of my platters in exchange.'

I had seen his platters in the gallery. Real works of art they were. I told him money was not the chief consideration. I would like to see the timber used.

'Right,' he said. 'Can I cut it here?'

I heard later that Paul never cuts down a tree. Such is his love of forests that he cannot bring himself to cut the trees. So a gift such as this, where nature had done the felling, was more than welcome.

It took him several days, and when he had cut all he could use and stacked it on his truck he gathered all the small branches and the foliage and carted them up the paddock, to be burnt later in the open fires we sit by on winter evenings. Knowing the good use to which Paul would put most of the timber, I did not feel guilty about burning the remainder.

Nine months went past. 'You'll never see him again,' said my sceptical husband. I was convinced that in this instance he would be proved wrong.

Then one morning there was a knock on the door and Paul stood there. In his truck was a young walnut tree in a pot, all ready to plant.

The surviving walnut is still
bare in early spring as the
daffodils and muscari come
into flower.

And in Paul's hands was the most beautiful platter – soft golden timber that felt like satin and had the most intricate grain. It was made from our walnut. Truly as Hans Knorr had written the great tree had 'run into resurrection underneath his hands'.

It sits permanently on the kitchen table, filled for much of the year with lemons. But in late summer when the quinces hang heavily on the trees like great golden globes the place of the lemons is taken by the quinces that I bring in to make jelly. Their strange, pungent scent fills the room.

Extending the shrubbery

The little flight of steps that led down from the lawn at the front of the house to the shrubbery ended abruptly beside a giant holly. While it was in itself distinctly grand and commanded a degree of respect, it had grown so big that it darkened the rooms on that side of the house and made growing anything nearby an impossibility.

We have an oversupply of hollies. There are two big ones beside the drive, two enormous ones far up beyond the stables and countless lesser ones in the paddocks. Most importantly there is Great-aunt Mary's holly, which we cherish. I hoped this one had no such history that would compel me to retain it.

Finally the decision was taken. If we wanted to extend the shrubbery the holly had to go. It was without doubt a job for an expert. No amateur could undertake a task of this magnitude. So the expert was called in and – not without regrets on our part – the mammoth tree was felled. Truckload after truckload of branches were carted up into the paddocks to be burnt in the winter. Then it was the turn of the stump muncher. He munched away happily for half a day, left a huge excavation and went on his merry way.

A few months later the remnants of stump sent out fresh green leaves. All our efforts had merely had the effect of a thorough pruning. The old tree was undeterred. After due consideration we painted the new shoots with undiluted Round-up. I have found this effective with elm suckers and the robinias that keep coming up in the lawn. It had no effect at all on the holly.

'Mme Grégoire Staechelin' bursts into bloom on the pergola at the
bottom of the steps leading down from the shrubbery. It flowers in early
spring at the same time as the paler pink, Australian-bred 'Carabella',
which makes a low hedge to separate the garden from the parkland.

Bill cut the lateral roots with the chainsaw. And they all sprouted anew. Then John came up with the idea of mixing what he described as a cocktail of Round-up, Brush-off (which the local farmers use on blackberry) and diesel oil. He drilled holes in the stump and in all the lateral roots he could locate, and poured this in. And the old tree acknowledged defeat. I felt like a criminal.

We waited six months before we attempted to plant anything in its vicinity. In the meantime we constructed broad stone steps, which lead down from the shrubbery to the lower lawn. We made a wide gravel path that curves from the foot of the steps and eventually gives access through wooden gates to the daffodil paddock. Over this path we erected five pergolas – sturdy wooden pergolas made of treated pine posts and lattice. Climbers are an indispensable part of a rose garden.

Apart from any other considerations I had to have something to support 'Mme Grégoire Staechelin', the aptly nicknamed 'Spanish Beauty'. This superb pink rose had clothed our veranda at Erinvale. She flowers only once, in spring, but it is an overwhelming sight and is followed in winter by huge golden hips, which in this cold climate eventually turn an orange red. I planted one on each side of the first pergola constructed, at the foot of the steps.

On the same pergola I planted the so-called Magnolia Rose, 'Devoniensis', which we had also grown at Erinvale in a similar situation. It is one of those roses that tends to hang its head, so is best looked up at from below. It is a Tea rose and the possums loved its young red shoots, so until – much later – we erected an electric fence right round the garden there was a constant battle, won as a rule by the possums. The electric fence defeated them in the end and the rose is now free to grow.

The fence was not erected with the possums in mind. Nor were we trying, as some of our neighbours thought, to discourage passers-by from climbing the fence to pick the daffodils. We had lost a young, very much loved, heeler on the Bass Highway and the electric fence was erected primarily to keep the dogs in. Quite fortuitously it appears also to keep the possums out.

On the second pergola I planted the very prolific 'Mme Alice Garnier', also known as 'Brownlow Hill Rambler'. She flowers later than the others and is a picture in early summer when she bears literally thousands of rather ragged little pink blooms. Her companion on this pergola is perhaps my best loved of all the Alister Clark roses, 'Cicely Lascelles'. (Of course as I write this I think of 'Editor Stewart' and 'Mrs Richard Turnbull' and 'Tonner's Fancy' and realise afresh that it is impossible to have a favourite.) This lovely climber – a warm, fresh pink – is also recurrent. For good measure I added the clematis 'Marie Boisselot' – pure white and sufficiently strong growing to give even Madam Alice a run for her money.

The third pergola is clothed with the very popular 'Constance Spry' and the equally well-loved clematis 'Nelly Moser'. Both of them are tall growing and vigorous and clamber up into the branches of the nearby grey-foliaged buddleja, 'Lochinch'. 'Nelly Moser' puts on a solo performance again in autumn when 'Constance Spry' is resting. On one corner of this pergola is what to me is the loveliest of all white climbers, the early Tea rose 'Sombreuil'. She displays nothing of the vigour of her companions so needs an extra measure of care, but she flowers recurrently and has probably the richest perfume of them all.

The fourth pergola is given over to the rampant apricot-pink 'Souvenir de Mme Léonie Viennot'. She could cover it quite happily with no help at all, but for good measure I planted with her a white wisteria.

A fifth pergola was something of an afterthought. We erected it at the top of the steps as I needed support for the much-loved red climber 'Château de Clos Vougeot' – a deep, dark velvety red, with a correspondingly rich scent. This is a rose I could not be without. Perhaps I had it in the garden already. The cuttings of Annie's rose from the sunny court-yard had struck but I had not yet seen a spring flowering. I had trouble finding two 'Château de Clos Vougeot' – and of course it is essential always to plant the same rose on each side of a pergola or archway. Eventually I succeeded and planted with them what has probably been the most successful of my large-flowered clematis, the lavender-blue 'Will Goodwin'.

A bed runs right along beside the pergolas from the foot of the steps to the gates into the daffodil paddock. In this I planted a collection of shrub roses – two or three of each. Alister Clark's so-well-named, semi-single, pale pink 'Daydream' is here. This can be treated as a shrub or a small climber. I have treated it as a shrub but bent the long canes horizontally to increase flowering. Having no hazelnut canes such as were used at Sissinghurst for this purpose, I acquired some of the thin metal posts used by the local farmers to erect movable electric fences. They have a large loop at the top and the rose canes can be threaded through.

Two of the early striped roses also found a place in this bed. I find it difficult to account for my love of the old striped roses and my dislike for most of the modern bicolours. Perhaps the colouring of the old roses is more subtle. 'Mme Driout' was released in France in 1902. It is a sport of the cherry-red 'Reine Marie Henriette', but 'Mme Driout' is pale pink with irregular stripes of the cherry red of her parent. The other striped rose I have included here is also French – the Bourbon 'Commandant Beaurepaire'. Released in 1874, it is a deeper pink, striped almost purple, tall growing and sturdy. Both of these treasures are recurrent flowering so make an important contribution to this part of the garden. Because they are so floriferous I felt happy to include the once-flowering but very spectacular modern shrub rose 'Fritz Nobis', released by the German firm of Kordes in 1940. It compensates in some measure for its once-flowering by setting quite a good crop of orange hips. Jack Harkness describes this rose as 'one of the most handsome shrubs in the world; the double pink flowers with their crinkled petals stand on the bush as if it were a flower shop'.

Opposite Wooden gates lead from the last pergola into the daffodil paddock. In the beds bordering the pergola walk, 'Bourbon Queen' and 'Fritz Nobis' put on a fine late-spring display after the white wisteria on the last pergola has finished. 'Souvenir de Mme Léonie Viennot', which shares this pergola with the wisteria, flowers almost incessantly until the end of autumn.

On the opposite side of the path is the two-toned pink and white shrub rose 'Erfurt' – one modern bicolour that I do like very much. It is another of Kordes's roses, put out in 1939. Once established this flowers almost continually so I put it between two plants of 'Bourbon Queen', which unlike most of the Bourbons flowers only in spring. Despite this I would always find a place for it. It sends out long canes (which would be excellent pinned down with the electric fence posts) that are covered in blooms for weeks in early summer. I have underplanted it thickly with *Campanula persicifolia*, which flowers at the same time – a combination I saw and admired greatly in the gardens at Port Arthur.

Behind these I put two of the tall-growing Alister Clark rose 'Sunny South'. Alister wrote in *The Australian Rose Annual* that he regarded this as his favourite of all the roses he grew at Glenara. It was growing at Forest Hall when we came – a very aged plant. It was released in 1918 – hence our plant could well have been fifty or sixty years old. It is tall – it was very popular as a hedging rose – and this one, growing right under the living-room window, almost obscured the light. Much as I love it and delighted as I was to find one of Alister's roses growing here, I felt it really had to be moved. We did need to see out of the window. But the plant looked too decrepit to move. So again I took cuttings. I knew they would take. And reluctantly I dug the old bush out.

It proved to be nearly as resilient as the holly for next spring up it came again. It had been growing on its own roots and was not easily discouraged. I got Bill to hack it out with the mattock. He must have missed a bit for the following spring there it was again. This time Bill used the bar and extracted the last remnant of root. I took the poor mutilated thing up to the oak paddock and planted it – without much hope but as an act of contrition. Against all the odds it shot again, and there it stayed until Philip Woodfield, who helps occasionally with heavier jobs, inadvertently sprayed it when dealing with the blackberry. But by then my cuttings had turned into fine little plants and I put two of them in a place of honour in the bed beside the pergolas.

Here too I planted 'Amadis', one of the few remaining Boursault roses. This one was released in France in 1829. It sends out long, lax, thornless canes of a remarkable chocolate brown and bears crimson-purple flowers over a lengthy period. In fact I can find at least one flower at almost any time from spring until autumn.

This pergola-covered walk marks the end of the more formal part of the garden – the part given over to beds and paths – and separates it from the parkland. I wanted to mark this division with a hedge. I considered lonicera – too fast and needs cutting too often – and box – too slow. Finally I settled on a rose hedge. I wanted something that would flower recurrently and would have few if any thorns so that keeping it cut would not be a penance. It also needed to strike freely from cuttings so that if I lost one I could easily replace it. And it had to tone with all the pinks and whites on the pergolas. Red was ruled out. So was yellow. In the end I opted for the Australian-bred, palest pink 'Carabella'. It was released in 1960 by the Sydney breeder Frank Riethmuller. It has not disappointed me. It is now something over a metre in height, flowers almost continually and succeeds in clearly defining the point at which garden becomes parkland.

The integration of the daffodil paddock

EVENTUALLY I TACKLED the problem of linking the daffodil paddock to the rest of the garden. The first and most obvious step was to remove the fence that divided it from the garden. This done, I turned my attention to the broken-down stone wall at the upper, north-east end. The stones were huge – much too heavy for us to lift – and the whole was badly infested with blackberry, ragwort and dock. Three applications of Round-up at three-weekly intervals discouraged these, although it was a couple of years before I was convinced that we had finally eliminated them. Then we pushed and dragged and shoved the stones into a rough semblance of a wall. The two-tiered hedge in the sunny courtyard had proved a great success so I decided to try something similar here. The rough stone wall would never be a thing of beauty. I wanted as much as possible to hide it.

Probably the best roses of all for hedging are the Rugosas. They have everything the gardener could want – attractive disease-free foliage, recurrent flowers (most of them), huge scarlet hips (many of them). They ask for little attention – the annual removal of dead wood, an occasional drink in unusually hot, dry weather and a periodic handful of fertiliser.

Opposite The hips of the Rugosas that I planted are a feature of the daffodil garden in autumn. Birds scatter the plentiful seed and many tiny seedlings come up each year.

In this situation I didn't want a formal hedge so along the top of our 'wall' I planted four each of *R. rugosa* 'Alba' (one of the best and purest of all white roses), 'Sarah van Fleet' (mid-pink and one of the first roses to flower in spring, although she sets no hips), 'Scabrosa' (magenta, with creamy stamens – the Royal Rose Society in England has planted it as a hedge along its road frontage) and 'Roseraie de l'Haÿ' (almost purple, rich and royal, and strongly fragrant, but sets few hips). And at the foot of the wall, because it is lower growing, I planted sixteen of the single, pale pink 'Fru Dagmar Hastrup', interspersed with the pink and white nerines I had dug up from the sunny courtyard where their colour was not what was required.

Between the roses, in the pockets left by the irregular placing of the rocks, I planted penstemons. They are a wonderful collection of colours that blend with the pinks and magentas of the Rugosas – 'Alice Hindley' (mauve and white), 'Midnight' (deepest purple), 'Hidcote Pink' and 'Apple Blossom' (both pink), 'Sour Grapes' (pale blue and green), 'Swan' (white), 'Evelyn' (deeper pink) and *P. serrulatus* (a spectacular blue flushed with violet). Both the penstemons and the roses flower for months and the penstemons ask for almost as little attention as the roses – just a hard cut back once they have finally finished flowering. This bank has given me as much satisfaction as anything in the garden.

Shortly after it was established I received as a Christmas present from my grand-daughters a delightful little rustic bird feeder. This obviously called for a position of honour.

The previous spring I had planted in a circle six *Prunus serrula*, which I love for their rich mahogany-coloured peeling bark. I had always intended to plant roses between them. Years ago when I was gardening at Bleak House a chance seedling had made its appearance under a bank of the Rugosa hybrid 'Schneezwerg', one of whose parents is reputed to be the pure white *R. bracteata*. 'Schneezwerg' blooms recurrently and bears small, bright scarlet hips. My seedling was in every way similar to its parent except for colour – it is a bright lipstick pink, not white. Most self-sown seedlings are of little worth but I was taken by this one and fostered it. When I left Bleak House I thought that was the end of it. Then a year or two ago I received from John Nieuwesteeg a parcel containing five plants of this seedling rose. My successors at Bleak House had decided to register and propagate it. It was now on the market as 'Bleak House'.

So I sent away for five plants of 'Schneezwerg' and I planted the pink and the white alternately between the prunus trees, leaving one space as an entrance to what has become a little secret garden. In the centre is the bird feeder and in the entrance space I put an iron rose arch. There are no climbing Rugosas so on the arch I planted the exquisite but very temperamental 'Souvenir de la Malmaison'. If she blooms here her lovely silvery pink flowers will be a bonus, a perfect entrance to the garden. If, as is so often the case, she balls in the bud and turns brown and mushy, she is far enough away from the main part of the garden for us to ignore her.

And here was the perfect place for Annie's rose. My seven little plants in the glasshouse had grown apace. I could plant one at the foot of each of the prunus trees and have one left over in case of loss. I have still not finally decided whether it is in fact 'Château de Clos Vougeot'. If it is not then it is a close relative. It is the same dark claret red but it seems to flower more generously. So I shall continue to call it Annie's rose and rejoice in the fact that it has found a new home in the garden it has graced for so long.

This completed the planting of the circular garden. I trust that the birds – of which we have so many – appreciate it. Each year sees the growth denser and the garden more private.

All of this went some way to linking the daffodil paddock to the garden. But it was all at the top of the slope and still left a large rectangular expanse, which was lovely in the spring when the daffodils turned it into a golden wonderland but very dull for the rest of the year.

After a lot of thought I decided to run a crab-apple walk from the wooden gate where the pergolas end right across the daffodil paddock to the lake. There were many reasons for choosing crab apples for such a walk. They are hardy and quick growing. They withstand frost. They are decorative for a considerable part of the year. In spring they cover themselves with blossom – and crab-apple blossom is quite enchanting. In summer they produce an abundance of fruit. In autumn many of them turn most wonderful shades of gold and russet and red. They need little pruning – just the removal of dead or crossing branches and a little judicious shaping. And for me, added to all these virtues, they brought back happy memories of the gardens at Bleak House and Erinvale for I had planted crab apples in both of these gardens.

The problem was, which of this very lovely and very extensive family to choose? I needed twenty – ten on each side of a wide central path. And of course it had to be twenty of the same. One of my favourites is *Malus floribunda*, the so-called Japanese crab apple. It will reach a good height – perhaps 8 metres – and its arching branches are bent low in spring with a mass of small, pale pink flowers that open from enchanting red buds. It was a favourite of Edna Walling, who wrote that it 'fits charmingly into the landscape . . . it is fairyland beneath this little tree when the red buds all along the branches begin to pop open showing their white petals in spring'. But for my purposes it might be too spreading. I needed something more upright. So I contented myself with the two *M. floribunda* I had already planted in other parts of the garden.

Next I considered the very popular *M. ioensis*. The small double flowers resemble those of a rambler rose, a reminder that the crab apple is after all a member of the Rosaceae family. And its autumn colour is outstanding. But I didn't really want pink. Certainly not if there was any prospect of its flowering with the late daffodils. And I wanted one with colourful apples and brilliant autumn tonings.

I also seriously contemplated 'Golden Hornet' for its white flowers and glowing golden fruit. It will always bring back memories of the glorious garden at Bolobek, where twelve trees were planted to form a crab-apple walk that ended with an exquisite small sculptured figure in the centre of a clearing. I saw it first when the trees were covered in blossom and there had been an unprecedented early fall of snow. We occasionally have snow in the garden. With Bolobek in mind, 'Golden Hornet' was the first crab apple I planted at Forest Hall.

In the end I settled on 'John Downie'. The flowers are white and single, opening from pale pink buds. The fruit is larger than that of many crabs and turns a brilliant orange scarlet. A large tree of 'John Downie' in full fruit is a truly dramatic sight. Twenty of them should be quite breathtaking when they meet overhead in several years' time.

Opposite The fruit of 'John Downie' – the variety I chose to form the crab-apple walk – are a vivid orange scarlet. When the trees have matured I will be able to make enough jelly to feed an army.

I had been tempted to plant 'Jack Humm' from New Zealand. Its large scarlet apples hang in bunches like cherries and are so hard that the birds tend to leave them alone and look elsewhere for food. When I first saw the large flocks of beautiful green Tasmanian parrots swooping into the garden intent on a feast I rather wished I had chosen 'Jack Humm'. I did plant a couple later, further down the slope, together with *M. trilobata* and *M. hillieri*.

In a few years' time when all my crab apples are bearing I can see that I will have to start making crab-apple jelly. I have a delicious recipe from the famous Ballymaloe Cooking School, which I obtained on a trip to Ireland. It calls for 1.4 kilograms of crab apples, which makes quite a few jars of jelly. You will also need 1.4 litres of water, a lemon and some sugar. Wash the apples and cut them into quarters. Do not remove the peel or core. Put them in a large saucepan with the water and the rind of the lemon and cook until they are reduced to a pulp. Then comes the fiddly bit. You must put the pulp into a muslin or fine cotton bag and let it drip into a large bowl overnight. Next day discard the pulp, and measure the juice before pouring it into a preserving pan or a large saucepan. Allow one cup of sugar to each 300 millilitres of juice and warm this sugar in the oven – don't forget to do this. Then add it, with the juice of the lemon, to the pan, and bring the lot to the boil, stirring gently until the sugar is dissolved. Increase the heat and boil rapidly for ten minutes. Pot the jelly immediately in sterilised jars. If you like you can add some fresh sprigs of mint or rosemary to the apples while cooking. Crab-apple jelly is delicious with lamb.

The crab-apple walk was planted in the winter of 1998. We cut a further wide section out of the hawthorn hedge, at the end of the walk, so that the lake was visible from this part of the garden. And here John built a flight of wide stone steps leading down to the water. Opposite, on the far bank of the lake, I planted five scarlet oaks.

One of the big problems with the daffodil paddock is that the grass must be left unmown for at least six weeks after the daffodils have finished flowering if we are to have any flowers next spring. At this time of the year the grass grows apace and reaches almost waist height before we can cut it, by which time the mower will no longer go through it and we have to use a slasher.

I thought that even a few mown paths would make it look slightly less wild. We mowed strips in front of the Rugosa bank, in the middle of the secret garden and down the crab-apple walk. As I was reluctant to sacrifice all the daffodils in the walk, John and I spent days digging the bulbs up by hand and transferring them to the oak paddock.

Then outside and in between the crab apples, the whole length of the walk, I planted the beautiful, unsophisticated-looking, single pink David Austin rose 'Dapple Dawn'. It is a sport of 'Red Coat' and both are ideal hedging roses, hardy and floriferous. I don't know where the name comes from. It is tempting to connect it to the lines from the poem by Gerard Manley Hopkins: 'I caught this morning morning's minion kingdom of daylight's dauphin dapple-dawn-drawn falcon.' But there is certainly nothing of the ferocity and destructive power of the falcon about this simple, cheerful child of the morning.

Next autumn I plan to plant a lavender hedge of *Lavandula dentata* the whole length of the walk, outside the roses, and a border of *Nepeta × faassenii* on the inside. We shall keep the walk closely mown, cut the lavender hard in January each year and the nepeta two or three times as the flowers die down, and do all we can to encourage the oaks on the far side of the lake.

Last year across the bottom of the paddock – the Bass Highway frontage – I planted ten *Cupressus torulosa*. All the colour and joyousness of the roses and the crab apples called for the serious dark green and perpendicular shape of cypresses. I remembered the role the cypress plays in Italian gardens and thought they might perform the same office here.

⸻◆⸻

Beulah

In whatever part of the garden I am working I come across plants that have come to me from either Beulah or Dunedin. Beulah is not a big garden – not much more than the typical suburban block – but every corner of it, every nook and cranny, is planted and planted not with everyday plants such as may be found in most garden centres, but with rarities. Only the best are given a place here. Anything that does not perform up to expectations is resolutely removed. I am reminded of that fascinating book *Better Gardening* by the English academic and gardener Robin Lane Fox. If you can grow a really good variety he argued, why settle for an inferior one?

Judy Humphreys, the owner of Beulah, grew up on the east coast of Tasmania at Coombend, an old house – she describes it as almost derelict – surrounded by an equally old garden, which her mother tended with love. It was a country garden – masses of roses, banks of irises and peonies. It was not a sophisticated garden. At that time there were none of the specialist nurseries dealing in rare plants such as Tasmania is renowned for today. It was stocked with cuttings given her by friends and seeds collected in other country gardens. But there were always flowers in both house and garden. And if there was nothing

Opposite The container garden behind the house at Beulah is full of treasures. Each plant is given the conditions that best suit it. The deep blue ceanothus is a splendid backdrop.

in flower Judy remembers great bowls of Kentish cherries used as table decoration.

Roses were a part of Judy's childhood. Her mother had a tray she loved as a little girl. It was painted with Redouté's roses. And the book entitled *Roses* put out in London in 1957 and containing twenty-four full-page glorious paintings by Pierre Joseph Redouté was one of her mother's treasured possessions. Outside Judy's bedroom window grew a Moss rose. Every spring her father would ask, 'Is the old Moss rose out yet?', and they would go together to look at it. But the roses growing in her mother's garden at Coombend were mostly Hybrid Teas. There was nothing else available at that time. It was not until the Heritage Rose Society was founded in 1978 in South Australia that old roses started to make their appearance in nurseries and gardens.

And in bookshops. The favourite – almost the only – garden book Judy remembers on her mother's shelves was *Australian Home Gardener* by Leslie Brunning, described by the editor as 'The only comprehensive Australian Gardening Book ever compiled'. Comprehensive it certainly was, with information regarding everything from 'The Ethics of Gardening' to 'The Home Vegetable Garden' to palms and ferns. And of course there was a chapter on 'The Rose', which concluded with 'A List of Good Roses'. Many of them are still available today – 'Lorraine Lee', 'Talisman', my mother's favourite 'Mme Abel Chatenay', 'Golden Ophelia', 'Château de Clos Vougeot'. But there were no coloured photographs. The day of the garden photographer had not yet dawned and illustrations were without exception black and white.

It was when she came upon one of the newer types of garden book – books with full-page delightfully coloured illustrations – that Judy fell in love with old roses. Inspired by this book, she sent in her first rose order, planted the bushes in her mother's garden, and became the first convenor of the Tasmanian branch of the Heritage Rose Society when it was founded contemporaneously with the South Australian branch. She became known as the Rose Lady.

Later when Judy and her husband and two small boys moved to Newry, between Longford and Launceston, she started to garden in earnest. The house at Newry, an early inn called the Jew's Harp, had been built in the 1830s. Its old water mill was still standing. The house was surrounded by splendid ancient trees – predominantly oaks and variegated elms. There were picturesque outbuildings like those at Forest Hall – a barn and stables. These were skilfully incorporated into the garden that Judy developed round the house. It covered perhaps 2 acres and Judy proceeded to collect 'every old rose I could find'. It was the garden of a romantic – narrow winding paths seemed to have no ending. Rambling roses climbed over buildings and up into trees. No straight lines. No bare earth. No perceptible edges to beds. She loved this rambling country garden: 'It had a happy feeling. People were comfortable in it.'

She became increasingly absorbed, spent more and more time in the garden. As the boys went off to school and university and her husband's work demanded more of his time, she could lose herself in the garden. It was at Newry that she established her first shade house and started importing seed of rare plants from overseas. The excess was sometimes sold off to local nurseries. Judy loves growing things from seed but permission has to be sought to bring seed and plants into the country and putting plants in quarantine is both expensive and time consuming. Gradually she did less of it.

There comes a time for change. It is not always planned or sought but quite suddenly one becomes aware of the need for it. So it was with Judy when Beulah came on the market. It is a Launceston landmark, a grand old house classified by the National Trust. From a gardener's perspective this was a massive change. Scaling down from 2 acres to half an acre meant a total rethinking of plans and objectives.

Beulah's garden was a shady one, dominated by a huge liquidambar in front (since removed) and by four magnificent limes growing just outside the fence. But Judy still planted roses – perhaps a hundred – for she could not live without the spinosissimas that are her favourites, especially 'Frühlingsgold', which grows beside the front drive. Climbing 'Lady Hillingdon' adorns the high front fence that cuts the garden off from the outside world.

She plants the roses she loves, regardless of space. *R. glauca* towers up in a narrow bed along the front veranda, a bed so shady that it is theoretically totally unsuitable for roses. *R. glauca* (formerly *R. rubrifolia*) is blissfully happy and has shot up and become entwined in a purple bougainvillea that flourishes here because it is protected from frost. In fact Judy grows a good many plants that are usually classed as frost tender: a jacaranda,

This magnificent iris was grown at Beulah from seed. *Opposite above* The largest of the circles that separate the plantings in the front garden of Beulah is floored with round sea pebbles. *Opposite below* Vivid red and gold lachenalia grow in a wooden trough.

daturas, plumbago and a heavily laden lemon tree. A dedicated gardener can usually find a solution. After all the garden at Newry had been becoming shady too as the trees Judy had planted approached maturity, yet the roses had been magnificent.

Perhaps it was the shadiness of the garden that prompted her to establish her amazing collection of hydrangeas, many of them grown from imported seed. I have, for instance, grown and loved *H. quercifolia*, the oak-leaved hydrangea. But the variety Judy grows, known as 'Snow Cap', leaves all others far behind with its great panicles of white flowers faintly tinged with pink. Magnolias are at home here too – 'Heaven Scent', 'Caerhayes Belle' and the flamboyant, outsized 'Star Wars'.

Judy loves variegated foliage, especially when the variegation is white rather than cream. She grows two of the rarer forms of *Sambucus* (the elderberry) and two variegated forms of pittosporum (perhaps the varieties known as 'James Stirling' and 'Irene Patterson') and also the dwarf pittosporum with purple-bronze leaves known as 'Tom Thumb'.

This love of variegated foliage, especially when used to light up dark corners, reminds me of the garden of Margery Fish at East Lambrook. So too does the row of fourteen carefully clipped lonicera 'soldiers' that march alongside one of the paths just as Margery Fish's 'pudding trees' did.

Except for the drive the whole of the area in front of the house is gardened. There are no lawns. This area is characterised by a series of circles – some of stone, some of brick, one of pebbles. Judy has always loved circular lawns – perhaps because the circle seems to suggest harmony and wholeness and completion. Perhaps it was prompted by the old millstone that Judy brought with her from Newry. Whatever the explanation, the circle seems to dominate the garden. She uses the millstone as a table and it is surrounded by a circle of bricks. To this has been added a collection of smaller millstones 'so it wouldn't be lonely', and just inside the front gate is a huge black iron whaler's pot filled with water plants. Judy used to go with her brother to clearing sales and built up a collection of grindstones and millstones.

Many of the circles in the front garden are constructed with handmade bricks, some of them imprinted with the convict arrow. Narrow paths lead the visitor from one circle to the next. The biggest is floored with pebbles – large, smooth pebbles washed by the sea.

Wide borders sometimes make it difficult to see individual plants. This construction of paths and circles brings every plant to the visitor's very feet.

Beside the house is a quite different garden presided over by the only piece of sculpture at Beulah – a bust of a young girl with flowers in her hair. Made in Austria at the turn of the century, she too is a romantic. She sits amid camellias and hydrangeas, the ornamental grasses that have become popular, rarities such as a purple-stemmed eucomis (where most are green), roses such as the spinosissima hybrid 'Irish Rich Marbled' and the dark red 'Sympathie', which climbs up the white wall of the house and stands out against the charcoal grey of the shutters and the deep purple of the viticella clematis 'Polish Spirit' that weaves its way through its stems. Along the front veranda beneath *R. glauca* grows a tradescantia with purple stems and foliage. And the heavy scent of lime trees and lilies fills the garden.

A narrow strip of garden runs the full width of the block behind the house. It is quite steep and terraced up to the back fence. This is essentially a container garden. The containers, like the millstones bought over the years from clearing sales, are a fascinating collection ranging from old terracotta to ceramics to aged wooden troughs, a legacy of the days when horses were housed in the stables at Beulah. Clematis are twined along the railings of the steps, up into shrubs and roses. In the containers are tiny bulbs, alpines, gentians, irises. Many of them are rare, grown from seed and tended patiently, sometimes for years, before they come into flower. In such comparative isolation each plant is seen to best advantage. Nothing is swamped by its neighbour. In their often brief moment of glory nothing will be overlooked. They might be lost in a larger garden. Here every one of them is known by name, given the conditions it needs and enjoyed to the full.

My mind goes again to Robin Lane Fox and his *Better Gardening*. 'Any gardening is better than none,' he wrote, 'but some ways of gardening are better than others. Better gardeners seem to sense which plant is best, how to find the best oak or primrose and how to place it for the best impression.'

Judy Humphreys is just such a gardener. Gardening to her is as much a mental as a physical or aesthetic challenge. She spends long evenings and wet winter days reading and learning and constantly planning, so that in the end she chooses only the best plants, gives them the best care and attention and finally is rewarded by seeing a garden that is as interesting as it is beautiful and a delight in every season of the year, from the superabundance of spring to the rich sights and scents of summer to the comparative austerity of winter.

It is well named, this tranquil garden. I had forgotten until Judy reminded me that Beulah in John Bunyan's epic work *The Pilgrim's Progress* is the land of heavenly joy, 'whose air was very sweet and pleasant . . . where they heard continually the singing of birds and saw every day the flowers appear in the earth'.

The stables

I HAD NOT ORIGINALLY intended to include the stables in the garden. The high dry-stone wall behind the ash trees cut them off from the lawn. The wide gateway on the meandering drive had given access to the nine horses that were once stabled there. I suppose there were nine – at any rate there were stalls and feed bins for nine. Between the wall and the stables was a courtyard almost totally obscured by thistles and blackberry – blackberry so thick as to make entry to the stables impossible. I despaired of ever cleaning it up and decided that the garden should stop at the stone wall.

But I found myself going back and back to the stables. The fine part stone, part timber building was full of history. It conjured up images of hay carts and drays, of the time when this was a bustling farm. I pictured the draught horses being brought in in the evening and the ponies for the children – I kept finding horse shoes in the garden, of every size from draught horse to shetland. So one day in autumn, when the three ash trees beside the wall were in all their golden glory, I took to the blackberry with secateurs and shears and hoe and carved a path through. And when I stood finally at the entrance to the stables and looked through the ash trees across the lake to the grandeur of the Western Tiers beyond, I knew that this had to be part of the garden.

I poisoned the blackberry – not once but on three successive occasions. I try not to use poisons but blackberry is impervious to anything else. Then Philip came with his versatile little machine, which he calls an excavator but which seems to serve many purposes.

He levelled the ground and laid white gravel, which instantly created an impression of order. By the time he left we had a splendid court-yard, part sunny and part shaded, and enclosed by the wall on two sides and by the stables on the third.

I had amassed over the years a collection of old coppers. These I positioned strategically against the front wall of the stables and in them I planted the cheerful little pink Alister Clark rose 'Suitor' to give a steady succession of blooms for months on end. And on the wall I planted the thornless climber 'Pinkie'. She was slow to take off in her first dry summer and has suffered spasmodically from mildew. I never can understand why mildew should come under dry conditions. One would expect the reverse.

A few weeks later I had occasion to go to Ross. This involves passing the fascinating Plume Antiques. I never drive past without going in 'just to have a look', for Plume Antiques stocks an apparently inexhaustible supply of early Tasmanian relics – Huon pine and blackwood furniture, household equipment, old prints, farm machin-ery. On this occasion I found two splendid church pews, 3 metres long and in perfect condition. Jeremy, the proprietor, and I have struck up a friendship over the past few years, so when I asked him to hold the pews for me until he found a table the same length he readily agreed. A sturdy refectory table was what I wanted, something I could leave

Opposite above The stables. On the right the ash trees overhang the courtyard, which has become an outdoor living area.
Opposite below Gradually the roses took over from the herbs in the garden I built to one side of the stables. On the right is a Ballerina apple tree, originally the focal point of the 'herb garden'. At the front is 'Stanwell Perpetual', edging the path, then Alister Clark's 'Cracker' and a seedling from 'Irish Rich Marbled'.

outside without fear of its disintegrating, something I need not paint or stain, something that would seat ten on occasions.

It was not a month later that Jeremy rang to say he would be up that afternoon with my pews and a table. It was a perfect match – made of oregon and therefore virtually unaffected by weather, 3 metres long and so solid that I found it impossible to pick up even one end. Luckily Jeremy had brought his father with him to help lift it off the truck.

It sits now in the stables courtyard with the pews and we have a perfect outdoor living space. But one thing inevitably leads to another. Once we had installed the barbecue there for use not only on sunny days but also on those glorious long evenings that are one of the joys of living in this climate, it was obvious that the sheltered, sunny area on the north-west side of the stables was the perfect place for a herb garden.

No matter how informal the rest of your garden may be, a herb garden cries out for a degree of formality. The area at my disposal was a large square with the north-west wall of the stables as one boundary. A low wall of natural rock formed the north-east boundary. On this wall I decided to plant the lovely, almost evergreen rambling rose 'Adélaide d'Orléans', which I had fallen in love with in David Ruston's garden in Renmark, South Australia. From tiny pink buds come delectable scented white flowers. The canes are long and lax and as happy trailing down as they are climbing up – what a marvellous weeping standard it would make.

On the wall of the stables I decided to try the creeper *Actinidia kolomikta*, grown for its foliage rather than for flowers. I saw it first in the rose garden at Sissinghurst and have wanted to grow it ever since. The deep green leaves turn paler green, with white and pink blotches. It needs the cold to colour well and I thought it would also appreciate the shelter and support offered by the stables wall. The one at Sissinghurst is espaliered against a mellow red-brick wall.

Two intersecting paths were laid to divide the area of the herb garden into four equal squares. Something was needed to mark the intersection and I chose one of the columnar Ballerina apple trees. The beds were edged with chives and parsley and I planted various sages and thymes, salad burnet and oregano, and in the middle of each square the little pink China rose 'Old Blush', also known as 'Parson's Pink'. One of the first roses to come to

Tasmania, it can still be found in the garden at Port Arthur and in many a country church-yard. No collection of old roses would be complete without it. Having decided on them, I could not wait to get budded plants from the growers when they became available in winter. Instead I visited a deserted churchyard outside Launceston and took cuttings. All of them struck and I value them more highly than I would any commercially grown plants.

Then, just as the herbs were beginning to flourish, Walter Duncan, a good friend and one of the big rose growers from South Australia, sent me six tiny plants of the exquisite 'Dunwich Rose'. Although I have grown and loved the spinosissima hybrids for many years, I was somehow unprepared for the delicacy of this little rose – or for the rapidity of its very prickly growth. The tiny single flowers open cream with just the faintest flush of pink and a cluster of yellow stamens. As they age they turn white and are followed by round, black hips.

At the time of their arrival I had no place ready for these plants. I also had six plants of 'Stanwell Perpetual' in pots. I could never plan a garden without this loveliest of all the spinosissimas, a chance hybrid found in an English garden. So I got Philip and his machine back again to make a wide path leading up past the end of the herb garden to the back of the stables. On one side of this path I planted the 'Dunwich Rose' and on the other 'Stanwell Perpetual'. The latter is well behaved and constantly in flower (as its name suggests). The same cannot be said for the 'Dunwich Rose'. It flowers only in spring – I don't mind that – but is threatening to take over far more garden space than I had ever intended it should have.

I had no sooner found space for these two than I had a visit from Angela Archer, who lives at Brickenden, one of Tasmania's earliest and loveliest homes, surrounded by an established garden. She brought me roots of a seedling of the superb 'Irish Rich Marbled', one of the best in the very special spinosissima family. There was nothing for it but to plant them in the herb garden behind 'Stanwell Perpetual'. When they flowered some were single, some double, some flushed pink, some almost white – seedlings seldom come true – but all were delightful and all of them have flourished and suckered and spread.

Then I found an enchanting little book called *Scots Roses* – of hedgerows and wild gardens – by a truly remarkable woman. Mary McMurtrie was born in 1902 and the book

was published in 1998 when she was 96 years old. It is copiously illustrated with delicate watercolours, all her own work. What's more, she is currently working on a new book to be called 'Flora of Scotland'. Mary McMurtrie's love of the roses of her Scottish homeland kindled afresh my own love of them. Our hedge of the deep, rich, purplish maroon 'William III' at Erinvale had been one of the features of the garden. So on the north-west side of the herb garden – the one not already given over to roses – I put six plants of 'William III' struck from cuttings so bound to sucker. These little roses are beset with vicious thorns and working with them is difficult to say the least. Budding can be painful and cuttings are often the only option.

Soon afterwards I came upon potted plants of the brilliant 'Single Cherry' and bought three with no thought of where I might plant them – the 'herb garden' had now been entirely taken over by roses, with only the apple tree resolutely holding its own. So 'Single Cherry' stayed for the time being in pots.

A visit to Tom at Lottah yielded three plants of a spinosissima hybrid I had read about but not seen – 'Glory of Edzell'. Unlike the 'Dunwich Rose', this one grows tall, with long arching canes beset in spring with white-centred, bright pink flowers. It is a glory indeed. I put them in as a group among the species roses I planted later in the daffodil paddock. Their ferny foliage makes them look quite at home in this company and I had run out of space in the 'herb garden'.

Then of course, having gone thus far towards a spinosissima collection, I felt I had to include *R. spinosissima* 'Altaica' (synonymous with *R. pimpinellifolia* 'Grandiflora'), with its glistening, simple single white flowers and its round, purplish black hips. I paid another visit to Tom. His is a fascinating nursery in the wild forest country of the north-east of the State. He is a true plantsman and stocks things not to be found elsewhere. Here I came upon what I was after. The 'herb garden' was by now overpopulated but there was no shortage of space in the daffodil paddock.

_____

Opposite The round black hips of the 'Dunwich Rose' are characteristic of the spinosissimas and attract much attention.

Beside
the barn

At the side of the house, separated by the drive from what used to be the kitchen garden, is the barn. The builders who carried out most of the renovations for us are convinced that it is the oldest building on the property. The bottom storey is of solid stone like the house. The two upper floors are of split shingles. The bearers that support the first floor are huge, roughly sawn tree trunks, clearly designed to last and to carry considerable weights. The narrow windows have no glass and look out onto the ancient viburnums, cotoneasters and japonicas in the shrubbery and across to the Western Tiers.

At the southern corner of the barn is the venerable mulberry tree. Previous owners had not treated it kindly. The great gnarled limbs had been hacked about so that the tree is now sadly misshapen. But it still bears each year a huge crop of luscious, juicy, deep purple mulberries, irresistible to all who pass beneath it. At its twisted feet, partly to disguise the butchery to which it had been subjected over the years, I planted *R. brunonii*, the Himalayan Musk Rose. After four years it has reached to the top of the mulberry tree and is preparing to scramble across to the barn. Its large clusters of little single white flowers are beginning to peep in through the top window in early summer and to fill the barn with their scent.

At the opposite end of the building a blue wisteria, with a trunk nearly as twisted and gnarled as that of the mulberry, has reached to the very ridge capping and hangs like a curtain across the windows. It flowers earlier than the rose, reaching its peak at the beginning of October.

I have never discovered what the barn was used for. The stairs that formerly must have led to the top floor have been removed, and there are only traces of the internal walls that must once have divided the barn into compartments. There was nothing left that might have indicated its original function – no stalls or feed bins as in the stables, no forge or bellows as in the blacksmith's cottage. But it is without doubt part of Forest Hall's history.

By the time we arrived the north-west wall was totally covered in ivy and the south-east wall with a banana passionfruit (*Passiflora mollissima*) vine. Ivy is notoriously destructive and this one had taken its toll on the wooden shingles, the insidious tendrils worming their way under and around them. The passionfruit vine was not much better. It spreads rapidly and uncontrollably and it was months before I was convinced I had finally got rid of it. No poisoning this time – just constant hand weeding.

The ground slopes down from the drive on the north-east to the barn, so the ramp that came out at right angles from the barn was at first-floor level. The slope down from the drive was dangerously slippery in wet weather or when iced over with frost, especially for gardeners wheeling barrows. The first thing we did was replace the ramp with a flight of steps hard against the barn wall. Then Philip came in with his excavator and levelled a path beside it. John, who would much rather do creative stonework than mow lawns, built another of his masterly dry-stone walls to retain the earth Philip had thrown up. Our slippery slope had, almost overnight, become a terraced garden. We now had a narrow bed alongside the barn, a gravelled path beside this, then John's wall and a much wider bed between it and the drive.

I was delighted. I was presented with two new beds as ideal for growing roses as our sunny courtyard is. They get sun for most of the day. The drainage is perfect. The soil is the rich red soil the local potato farmers love. And the barn is the perfect backdrop for a rose garden.

The rosy red-brick walls in English gardens are something I have hankered after for years – walls that traditionally enclose kitchen gardens or picking gardens, with vines or fruit trees espaliered on them. We don't quite have that but the convict-built barn is a suitable substitute. Against it I had planted, in our first winter, the pink climber 'Awakening'. It had flourished and was well on the way to the second storey. It is a sport of the deservedly

An ancient wisteria climbs up
the shingle wall of the barn, right
to the ridge capping. Beneath it
is a mass of *Arum italicum*.
Opposite above In the barn
garden roses are underplanted
with foxgloves, species
geraniums, campanulas and
bulbs. *Opposite below*
Clematis armandii 'Apple
Blossom' has been planted on
the lattice of the barn steps.

popular 'New Dawn' but it is more double and a paler pink than its parent. It has many admirers, although I have to confess I prefer 'New Dawn'. However, it had got away to such a good start in life that I hadn't the heart to replace it. So it set the colour scheme for the rest of this garden.

There was room for one more climber here and after a good deal of thought I decided on *R. anemonoides*, the 'Anemone Rose'. This is a warm pink version of the glorious pure white *R. laevigata*, the 'Cherokee Rose'; I have not planted this here because I had a singular lack of success with it at Bleak House. It hated the cold and while its glossy dark green foliage was a delight it seldom produced a perfect bloom. In most years, due to severe late frosts, it produced none at all. So it was with grave misgivings that I decided to plant *R. anemonoides*. But the spot allocated to it is right against the wall, bathed in sunshine for most of the day, protected from frost and from the prevailing winds. In the very first year it produced half a dozen single, glowing pink blooms, faintly tinged with mauve, that opened flat to golden stamens. It has the added virtue of flowering recurrently, where *R. laevigata*, if conditions suit it and it deigns to flower at all, does so only in spring.

The steps that run up beside the barn provided another support for a climber. I decided to clothe them with the evergreen *Clematis armandii* 'Apple Blossom'. Even in its second spring it covered the railings with an abundance of exquisite starry, palest pink flowers, which hung on through the whole of September and into early October before any of the roses were in flower. *R. anemonoides* flowers much earlier than 'Awakening', which delays its performance until mid-November but then continues over a long period. The combination of these three, helped by the early-flowering wisteria, means that the barn is a picture throughout spring.

In front of the climbers I wanted some tall shrub roses – partly to hide the stems of the clematis, which can become very untidy. Because of the suggestion of mauve in *R. anemonoides* I chose the Hybrid Musk rose 'Lavender Lassie'. Unlike most of the widely grown Hybrid Musks, this one was not bred by the Reverend Pemberton but by Kordes, the German firm. It blooms continually from spring until the end of autumn, and in colour it is just the lavender pink I was looking for. I planted two and would have liked three but this bed is not wide and space is limited.

The next choice was the Alister Clark rose 'Mrs Fred Danks'. As is the case with many of Clark's roses, the parentage is not known but it must be one of his greatest successes. It grows tall and flowers abundantly – perfectly shaped flowers of a true lilac pink.

In front of these tall-growing roses I decided to plant the low-growing 'Lavender Pinocchio'. Released in 1948 in the USA, it has retained its popularity partly because of its unique colouring and partly because it flowers so prolifically and is excellent for picking. It seldom grows above 60 centimetres.

Towards the end of the bed I wanted to move away from the lilac tones and return to the clearer pink of 'Awakening', so I planted two of the early Tea rose 'Duchesse de Brabant'. This French rose has been loved by generations of gardeners since its release in 1857.

At the very end of the bed I put two plants of 'Gruss an Aachen', chosen for its delightful shape (flat and many petalled), its colour (a rich ivory white delicately flushed with pink) and its heady scent. David Austin thinks so much of it that although it was bred in Germany he pays it the compliment of regarding it 'as an ideal English Rose'. I can't help wondering if its German breeder, Philipp Geduldig, would have regarded this as a compliment. He had named it for Charlemagne's capital city.

In the last available space I tucked in the little China rose 'Le Vésuve'. This eventually forms a bushy shrub and, like many of the Chinas, blooms almost incessantly – displaying perfectly shaped flowers that vary from a deep pink to a colour very similar to that of 'Duchesse de Brabant', which grows beside it.

The making of the second of the two beds beside the barn has been a real delight. I have forgotten who it was who said that it is the journeying and not the arriving that gives the greatest joy, the making and not the thing made. Certainly I have found it so with each new project undertaken. This bed was no exception.

In shape it is a large rectangle sandwiched between the white gravel drive on the upper side and the new gravel path on the lower, with the barn as backdrop. Gardens and buildings must be in harmony with each other. A formal garden with standard roses and box hedging would not have been in keeping with the barn. It called for something simple and unsophisticated, looking almost as though it had come about by chance.

When I first started to grow roses I loved some of the great, voluptuous double

blooms. I remember planting the Hybrid Perpetual 'Paul Neyron' at Bleak House and being enthralled by its outsized, rich pink blooms. Later I read a description of it written by the English rosarian the Reverend Foster Melliar: 'giant blooms stout in petal and very full . . . wanting in delicacy'. I am forced now to agree with him. The more roses I grow, the more I love the single ones. I think I am not alone in this. So in planning the bed in front of the barn I settled after much thought on a collection of singles and semi-singles in pinks and whites to harmonise with the ones planted in the first bed.

I sought for and found 'White Wings'. It bears single, purest white flowers, with rosy brown stamens. The bush grows to something over a metre in height and the flowers are borne in clusters. I have grown 'Golden Wings' for years and love it dearly, and had always intended to plant 'White Wings' too. Here was the opportunity.

Surprisingly the two are not related, although both were bred in the USA. 'White Wings' is the result of a cross between the popular 'Dainty Bess' and an unknown seedling. I grew 'Dainty Bess' years ago and loved its single, soft pink flowers, with their deep maroon stamens. As I had decided on single and semi-single roses for this bed these two seemed the perfect choice, although I had found 'Dainty Bess' finicky and difficult. Perhaps she will do better under the perfect conditions offered to her here. I planted three along the back of the bed above the stone retaining wall, and one of 'White Wings' at each end.

On the side adjacent to the drive I planted four of the modern cluster-flowered rose 'Seduction'. The semi-single flowers have pretty, wavy petals. They are white, edged and flushed with pink, and borne over a very long period. They last wonderfully well when picked.

Opposite The grey shingle wall of the barn is a fine backdrop for this sea of colourful lupins and the pink Tea rose 'Mme de Tartas' in the garden that was once devoted to vegetables. The lupins have grown so high that from a distance they obscure the barn garden. *Following pages left* Euphorbia myrsinites trails over John's retaining wall. If we are lucky its flowering coincides with that of the dark blue muscari.   *Following pages right* David Austin's 'Scepter'd Isle' grows tall and flowers prolifically over a very long period.

It is remarkable how many really lovely roses have come about by chance. Most rose growers will know the story of the discovery of the beautiful semi-single, pale pink 'Souvenir de St Anne's' in a garden outside Dublin – a sport of 'Souvenir de la Malmaison'. It is the same blush pink as its parent but holds its shape much better and flowers more reliably. Many rose lovers would list it among their favourites. I planted four in this new bed.

On each corner I wanted a slightly deeper-coloured rose. I chose David Austin's 'Canterbury'. Its breeder considers it 'one of the most beautiful of the single or near single roses other than the Species Roses'. It is a positively glowing pink, with the spicy scent we expect of David Austin's roses. The bush is low and spreading, not much above a metre in height, and it flowers continually.

A garden such as this – flat and of a regular shape – demands a centrepiece. In a different situation and without the dominating presence of the barn one might consider a birdbath or a fountain or a weeping standard rose. None of these would be in keeping with the atmosphere generated by the barn so one by one they were ruled out. Finally I settled on another of the Ballerina apple trees, the one named 'Flamenco'. It grows tall and straight and columnar. It will not take up too much room or cast too much shade – and the flowers are white splashed with pink. Nor will it be so susceptible to wind damage as a weeping rose might be.

With the roses in place I turned my thoughts to the underplanting. First on my list were the cranesbills, the true geraniums. On the slopes of Mt Wellington outside Hobart I found a nursery, called Plant Hunters, that specialises in exotic perennials and advertises a wide range of cranesbills. From them I acquired 'Johnson's Blue', which is not unlike *G. himalayense*. It bears large, violet-blue flowers over a long period, starting in early spring. It grows to approximately 30 centimetres. Anything much taller than this can be a nuisance under roses. Not unlike this one is *G. × magnificum*, also a deep violet blue and with foliage that displays rich autumn colour. But this one ultimately grew too tall and got tangled up with the roses.

From David Glenn at Lambley Nursery in Victoria I got a beautiful pale blue one, which he had named for his artist wife 'Criss Canning'. And from Norgate's in Trentham, Victoria, I got a splendid parcel containing *G. ibericum*, another deep blue cranesbill, which grows to little over 20 centimetres, the soft lilac-coloured *G. macrorrhizum* 'Ingwersen's Variety' and the gentle *G.* × *oxonianum* 'Wargrave Pink'. Perhaps the one that gives me most pleasure is a low-growing cranesbill with unusual, very double, deep blue-purple flowers. The label says 'Birch Double'.

Along the top of the retaining wall I put a few clumps of the prostrate *Euphorbia myrsinites*, which has attractive bluish grey foliage and lime-green flowers. Its prostrate habit encourages it to trail down over the wall. It flowers in late winter and very early spring and coincides with the deep blue muscari – a spectacular and easy-care combination.

This completed the permanent planting and I filled the gaps with dwarf foxgloves, dwarf delphiniums and blue lobelias. As the years go by and the permanent plantings become firmly established I probably won't need the 'fillers', although I would always find a spot for foxgloves – white and apricot and pink and mauve and all the shades between – in fact already by their second year they had seeded generously in the bed, in the gravel path and in the bed on the other side.

A very
special
garden

JUST BEFORE CHRISTMAS 1999 I had occasion to make a very special garden in memory of the dear four-footed friend who had gardened with me on a daily basis for just on fifteen years.

His youth had been spent at Bleak House, where he had had free range of the garden and surrounding paddocks, leaping the fences with such agility that Bill nicknamed him Moss Trooper after the Irish steeplechaser. On Sunday evenings he and his brother would swim across to the island in the middle of the big dam when we rowed across to water the trees planted there. Then they would jump, wet and dripping, into the boat to be taken back.

He loved the years he spent at Erinvale, his chief joy being the daily advent of the postman. He would lie in wait at the bottom of the drive and as soon as he heard the bike he would rush to the highest corner of the garden to accompany him along the fence to the mailbox, barking vociferously all the way.

He travelled with me always in the car, sitting on the front seat challenging all comers but ducking his head whenever a big truck came towards us. He accompanied me on the long interstate trips I made when I was gathering material for *Rose Gardens of Australia*. Mostly he slept in the car but once or twice a sympathetic motel owner allowed him inside. Sometimes he was called upon to play a more active role – as on the day I drove out to Durham Hall only to find the gate blocked by a mob of steers. All his inbred herding instincts came to the fore. I let him out and within minutes the driveway was clear.

He didn't much care for the flight to Tasmania – he hated the indignity of being confined in a wire cage and manhandled by strangers. But once here he loved it. He had his own apartment in the upper floor of the barn, where the wisteria hung in through the windows and little birds nested in the rafters above his head.

He was overjoyed when Bill bought the four-wheeled motorbike for use in the garden. For him it took the place of the postman's bike and he accompanied me every time I rode the bike and trailer up into the paddock to dispose of garden rubbish. He gardened with me every day, lying in the shade near where I was working and watching my every move. I miss his company more than I can say, so when we lost him I decided to dedicate to him one special corner of the garden he had loved.

I had not originally intended to extend the 'herb garden' behind the stables or include the slope beyond in the larger garden. But it was open and sunny – and it had been one of his favourite places. Here he had been wont to sit, looking across the lake and the fields – fields of corn, delicate mauve poppies grown for the pharmaceutical companies, white pyrethrum – and thence to the deep blue of the Tiers. There are huge rocky outcrops here, covered in moss and silver-grey lichen – the sort that costs a fortune if bought from a landscape supplier. They formed a natural backdrop to the bed that became his garden.

Red roses had to be the main feature. He was such a masculine dog – father, in his time, of twenty-one beautiful puppies. His coat was a deep metallic blue and he had a white star on his satin-smooth head and the characteristic markings of the well-bred heeler – a brown bar across the chest and quizzical brown eyebrows. Pink roses would have been out of place for such a fellow. So I looked for red roses. I wanted recurrent flowering ones to ensure that there would be colour here for as much of the year as possible. I wanted roses with scent, deep red roses that would not fade in the sun. And I wanted something that included his own name. There is 'William III', the dear little almost-purple spinosissima we used for a hedge at Erinvale. But the flowers are small and borne only fleetingly in spring. And I had already planted a border of them in the 'herb garden'.

In the end I settled for David Austin's 'William Shakespeare'. I think it is one of the best of Austin's reds and it reminds me of one of my all-time favourites, 'Charles de Mills'. But where 'Charles de Mills', being a gallica, bears its superb blooms only in spring,

'William Shakespeare' blooms recurrently. It is not easy to find rose plants in December and of course I did not want to wait until the following winter. However, a search rewarded me with two superb plants in pots, already well established and in bud.

Ostensibly Willy had been Bill's dog, although I don't think he ever realised it. He loved us both equally and unequivocally. Since Bill's passion in life is fly-fishing, I sought for and found a fine plant of the dark red 'Fisherman's Friend'. This filled all my requirements. David Austin described its colour as a 'deep garnet-crimson' and its scent as 'a powerful "Old Rose" fragrance'.

As a border I planted the soft silver-grey, lacy-leaved *Artemisia canescens*, which I had grown at Erinvale along the top of the stone walls, and in the middle of the bed the taller *A. ludoviciana*. This comes from Mexico and is completely frost hardy. I chose the variety known as 'Valerie Finnis', named after the famous English alpine expert. It spreads rapidly – can even become something of a pest if given free rein – and needs cutting back before the flowers form. The decorative foliage of the grey *Chrysanthemum haradjanii* from Turkey guaranteed it a place – like 'Valerie Finnis', it needs its buds cutting off before the rather harsh yellow flowers appear. At the back of the bed I put macleaya, the plume poppy, which can sometimes reach a height of 2 metres. The beautiful grey-green foliage is almost white underneath. And I included the spectacular *Papaver orientale* 'Beauty of Livermere' – brilliant red, with a black centre. As well, I found seed of the scarlet Californian poppy. It germinates only fairly and is not nearly so hardy and apt to self-seed as the yellow, cream or orange varieties. Among them I planted *Cerinthe major* 'Purpurascens', its blue-green leaves spotted white, and its purple bracts almost navy blue – a marvellous foil for the dark red roses.

I also included the scarlet geum 'Mrs Bradshaw' and deep purple *Campanula glomerata*. And *Veronica spicata* subsp. *incana* for the clumps of silver-grey foliage it forms, and the more temperamental *Mertensia asiatica*, with its tubular, pale blue flowers that open from delicate pink buds. And I found a strange species gladiolus called *G. papilio*, which comes from the Transvaal and bears beige flowers marked reddish purple.

I wanted a plaque for this very special garden – something to mark it as Willy's. Deloraine is a centre for craftworkers: for potters, sculptors and silversmiths, woodcarvers and painters. Its annual craft fair brings thousands of visitors to the town from all over the island and from interstate. I sought out Carol Ward, who paints on wood. Carol comes from England and calls her very creative small business Lindum Country after the part of England that was her home. I explained what I wanted: something not too big, with Willy's name and dates and a small inscription, surrounded by flowers – a garden in fact, dominated by red roses. It needed to stand up to the weather and have legs that could be tapped into the ground to hold it firm.

I picked it up a week later and was delighted. Carol had used treated pine so that it would not rot away, and she had covered the finished article with several coats of a clear lacquer to preserve the paintwork. And it was a garden. On a background of dark green she had painted dark red roses with tiny lilac-blue violas and white daisies – pyrethrum perhaps?

So I put in several plants of *Viola cornuta* around the plaque. It spreads by rhizomes and bears its deep blue flowers through spring and summer. And I included our own little native violet, *V. hederacea*, which suckers and spreads quickly, forming a dense mat. Its white flowers with a lilac throat are borne for months on end.

We really needed no memorial for Willy. Such a faithful friend is never forgotten. But this little corner of the garden might be seen perhaps as a mark of gratitude for years of love and companionship.

Willy's plaque.

Here, from the slope behind the stables, where Willy's garden is,
Forest Hall is seen in winter. The roof was painted blue to match the
blue of the Western Tiers – snow capped at this time. On the right is
the towering linden, and the tops of the two cedars in front of the
house are also visible.

Willy's garden extended

SLOWLY AND WITHOUT my intending it, Willy's garden crept up the hill. 'William Shakespeare' and 'Fisherman's Friend' bore such a succession of royal blooms that I could not resist the temptation to plant more reds. The first to be added was 'Othello' – two large vigorous plants. And what a splendid name for this passionate dark red beauty. Then came 'L. D. Braithwaite', which David Austin regards as 'the brightest crimson among the English roses', and 'Noble Anthony', which is something of a disappointment – a pinky red that looks washed out beside the others. I was glad I had planted only one instead of two or three.

The Alister Clark roses were doing particularly well. The colder climate of the island appeared to suit all of them. The *R. gigantea* hybrid 'Mrs Richard Turnbull', which I had planted elsewhere in the garden, had reached 5 metres in a couple of years and covered itself with glorious single white roses in spring. I was encouraged to plant more.

My first selection for this red bed was 'Editor Stewart', which has to be one of the best reds I know. I think Alister thought so too as he experimented for years before he found one among his seedlings that he thought was good enough to be named for his great friend the editor of the *Australian Rose Annual*. It grows tall. In fact it could be treated as a pillar rose. The colour is a bright cherry red and the large, open flowers have unusual wavy petals. The young foliage too is red. I planted three and beneath them several plants of the achillea 'Cherry Pie'. I have been wary of planting achilleas because the common white one grows rampant in our paddocks and has proved difficult to eradicate. But I am assured that the cultivated varieties are much easier to control. In fact they need little attention other than a quick trim when they have finished flowering. And 'Editor Stewart' is sturdy and well able to contend with a little competition.

The other Alister Clark I decided to include here was 'Restless'. Its heavily scented, semi-single, dark velvety red blooms are borne all through spring and summer. Not much is known about its parentage but I think the name must have been chosen to indicate its very recurrent flowering. There is scarcely a break between flowers.

Colour was my first consideration in this bed, not type. So I did not hesitate to include among the modern shrubs one of my old favourites, 'Tuscany Superb'. And superb it is. It is a sport of the gallica rose 'Tuscany', which is thought to have come from Italy, perhaps as early as 1500. Known as the Old Velvet Rose, it is deepest darkest purplish red, with pronounced golden stamens and a rich scent. 'Tuscany Superb' was released by the firm of Paul in the UK in 1848 and is worth a place in any garden. The foliage is strong and a deep green. There are few thorns. Of course it flowers only in spring, but in a bed such as this where most of the roses are recurrent its outstanding spring performance justifies its inclusion.

Neither could I leave out 'Rosa Mundi'. An ancient rose, a sport of *R. gallica* var. *officinalis*, the Apothecary's Rose grown by the monks for medicinal purposes, 'Rosa Mundi' (*R. gallica* 'Versicolor') is one of the loveliest of the old striped roses. It is striped crimson and white. It too flowers only in spring so I returned then to the David Austin roses and put in three plants of 'Tradescant'. This is almost as dark and compelling in colour as 'Tuscany Superb' and is quartered like many of the old roses. It could in fact pass for an old rose. As 'Tradescant' is low and spreading, I put the bushes near the edge of the bed.

'Rosa Mundi' has romantic associations. It is said to have been named after Fair Rosamund, the mistress of Henry II. 'Tradescant' is named for the John Tradescants, father and son, who were both gardeners and plant hunters and were responsible for bringing many now familiar plants to England. (Many of us still grow tradescantia in shady corners of our gardens.) The two Johns were gardeners to Charles I, and among other things were responsible for the planning and design of two of the great English gardens now associated with the name of the Marchioness of Salisbury, Cranborne Manor and Hatfield House.

In 1977 the Tradescant Trust was established to commemorate these remarkable men and their tomb can be visited in the gardens of the church of St Mary-at-Lambeth, home to the Museum of Garden History.

Next I planted three of the 'Duchess of Portland', the Portland Rose, an important old rose that was brought to England by the Duchess of Portland near the end of the eighteenth century. It is also known as 'Scarlet Four Seasons' as it is thought to be related to 'Quatre Saisons', the Autumn Damask. From the Portland Rose originated a small group called the Portlands. Two of the group – 'Comte de Chambord' and 'Jacques Cartier' – are still available and quite widely grown because, like the Portland Rose itself, they are recurrent. My three little plants settled in quickly and bore their perfumed scarlet blooms sometimes streaked with white all through summer and autumn.

I have grown the Hybrid Tea 'John S. Armstrong' for many years and value it highly for its strong growth and its steady succession of fragrant, clear red blooms, which last well when picked. So I put in three and beside them the David Austin rose 'Red Coat'. The latter's individual, almost single flowers are not striking but the bush grows tall and when covered in blooms (which it frequently is) makes a great sight. I planted three and in the middle of the group the red clematis 'Corona', which is scrambling up among them very enthusiastically. They want something deep purple as a groundcover – possibly *Campanula poscharskyana* or another clematis: 'Jackmanii Superba' perhaps, which is a strong, velvety purple and flowers from summer to autumn.

I found a spot for 'Souvenir d'Alphonse Lavallée'. It is usually classed as a Hybrid Perpetual but some experts, including the greatest expert of them all, Graham Thomas, think it has more of the characteristics of the Bourbons. It is a lovely, scented, deep crimson-purple rose. It flowers recurrently and is often grown as a small climber. I had wondered about the identity of Monsieur Lavallée and discovered recently that he was an amateur dendrologist and highly thought of. He was responsible for the creation of a herbarium containing some 4000 species. For this information I am indebted to the American rosarian Brent Dickerson.

I could find only one plant of David Austin's 'Tess of the d'Urbervilles'. I had read Thomas Hardy's novel of this name first as a schoolgirl, later as a student and several times since, never tiring of its passion and tragedy. The dark red rose that bears Tess's name reflects something of this; something of the darkness and sorrow that pervaded her life and is so typical of Hardy's work.

There was a sudden leap then to the present day with the addition of two sturdy plants of 'Scarlet Queen Elizabeth', a cluster-flowered floribunda released by Dickson in 1963. Its brilliant, almost orange scarlet – a colour never found in old roses – makes it difficult to place among the darker, more purple reds, but I have surrounded it with the navy-blue *Cerinthe major* 'Purpurascens', scarlet eschscholzia and the achillea 'Paprika' – and I might just get away with it. 'Scarlet Queen Elizabeth' is, like its parent, the popular pink 'Queen Elizabeth', very tall growing so beneath it I put three plants of Meilland's 'Red Meidiland', which grows almost prostrate and bears in clusters masses of little single scarlet flowers, with a white eye and pronounced yellow stamens.

This brought the bed right up to the back door of the stables. A space hard against the back wall was then planted with purple-blue echium, which need protection from our severe frosts. In front of them I put three plants of the Rugosa rose 'Delicata', which is an unusual soft lilac in colour, and in front of these *Lavandula dentata*, which seems to need trimming only once a year. The bed is edged with prostrate rosemary.

For Christmas that year I was given a copy of Beth Chatto's inspirational book *Beth Chatto's Gravel Garden*. It came at an opportune time just as I was concentrating on the underplanting for the red roses. This slope is open and sunny and well drained, and the soil is extraordinarily stony. After reading Beth Chatto's book I decided to try a collection of sedums. I have grown 'Autumn Joy' ('Herbstfreude') for years and love not only the flowers but also the seedheads, which turn rusty brown and hang on until you cut them off as the new shoots are making their appearance. Now I planted 'Ruby Glow'. The foliage is an attractive blue-grey and the flowers the colour of mulberries and cream. The purple foliage of 'Vera Jameson' made it a welcome addition – and its low growth made it doubly welcome. I was delighted also to find the sedum aptly named 'Frosty Morn'. I would grow it for the foliage alone. The combination of steely grey and cream makes it ideal for this area. I wanted *S. spectabile* 'Brilliant' as well because there is a wonderful photograph of it in Beth Chatto's book. So I turned to that unfailing source of information the *Aussie Plant Finder* and found the cultivar listed under two Tasmanian nurseries, Wychwood at Mole

Creek, and Woodbridge south of Hobart, from whom I regularly receive plants by mail order.

And here I stopped. *Stachys lanata* (which goes by a whole collection of names – lamb's ears, lamb's tongues, lamb's tails, woundwort) found its way in later and helped to fill the gaps. Also the curry plant (*Helichrysum italicum* subsp. *serotinum*), with its strange pungent scent. I wanted it simply as a groundcover but the young leaves can actually be used to flavour salads.

No doubt I shall continue to add more sedums and more grey-foliaged plants – even more red roses to the bed. It is indisputably the most colourful in the garden. I find it difficult to believe there was a time when I didn't much like red.

A shady courtyard

TALL FRENCH DOORS open from the sitting room into a courtyard on the southeast – elegant doors, with the original glass intact and the cedar panelling surrounding them untouched by paint. The courtyard is formed by the side of the main house and the kitchen wall that juts out at right angles to it.

Above the kitchen window looking into the courtyard is a delightful semicircular opening that was the only source of fresh air for the convict quarters above – those four tiny dark interconnecting unlined rooms. The solid stone chimney beside the kitchen must have provided the rooms with their only warmth.

The chimney and that wall of the kitchen are covered by the most attractive but very unruly variegated ivy that I had hacked into when I began my work on the shrubbery. I don't want to remove it totally, but each year when it reaches the eaves again and starts to clog up the guttering we give it a hard prune.

The courtyard itself was a sea of Japanese anemones, alstroemeria and valerian when we came to Forest Hall. A lovely foundation for a wild garden, although not really what I wanted here. Nevertheless, if we hadn't paved the courtyard, I feel sure they would be there still. But the builder who was carrying out the renovations in our first year insisted that paving was essential if we were to have any chance of keeping the cellars dry.

It is hard – and certainly unwise – to argue with experts when one's own knowledge of the field is decidedly limited. Accordingly we followed his advice. We used old bricks – the builder wanted new ones, but this was a matter of aesthetics not plumbing and

I won the day. And in the middle I insisted on having a square, 2 metres by 2 metres, left free. I wasn't sure what I wanted to put in it. But I was quite sure I wanted somehow to break up this sea of brick. In the event, either because of the paving or because the site is naturally well drained, the cellars have proved to be quite dry. And very useful.

The south-east side of the courtyard abutted the shrubbery. Here was an enormous old camellia. At least the bush was enormous – the flowers were quite small, although beautifully formed and very plentiful. Beside it was an almost equally huge bush of *Teucrium fruticans*, which we gradually clipped into shape, keeping some of the prunings to make future hedges. It strikes very easily from cuttings.

An outsized *Tamarix pentandra* towered over everything in that part of the shrubbery and threatened to become enmeshed in the powerlines. We cut it back – a process that it didn't resent at all – and it is a joy in spring when it is covered with feathery pink blooms. Under and around it are very large hydrangea bushes of a wonderful deep blue. I took cuttings from these too and used them later in other corners of the shrubbery.

There was also a beautiful deutzia and two bushes of the little pink rose 'Bloomfield Abundance', which is almost indistinguishable from the Sweetheart Rose, 'Cécile Brunner', except that the bush grows very much taller. It must have been many a long year since these two had seen the secateurs: they were quite out of control and growing in almost total shade. Yet, after the fashion of roses, they persevered and still bloom every year.

This must originally have been the most cultivated part of the garden for we found a low wall expertly built of cut stone. And an ancient tree peony extending its branches into the roses and the tamarix. Straggly and impoverished, it bore nevertheless great double pink blooms – a real boudoir pink – that filled me with tremendous excitement in our first spring. Tree peonies were things to be treated with respect where I came from – treasures to be nurtured with care.

Opposite The shady courtyard is a popular place on hot days. The semicircular fanlight above the kitchen window belongs to the one-time convict quarters.

That year, as he usually does, Bill asked me what I wanted for Christmas. I can seldom, offhand, think of an answer to this question. So he suggested I look for 'something useful for Forest Hall'. The following week I was entertaining a visitor from the mainland. Fishing was not one of her hobbies and she didn't much care for gardening either. So we visited the antique shops. In one of them I found a delightful little stone statue – a charming boy, his coat collar turned up against the cold, one hand thrust, in a manner reminiscent of Napoleon, into the front of his jacket. He stood well over a metre in height. I wasn't sure that he complied with Bill's suggestion that I buy 'something useful' but I was quite sure that he was exactly what was needed in the courtyard. So we arranged on the spot for him to be delivered to Forest Hall – he was too heavy for us to lift – and the following week he was installed in the centre of the square left in the paving. I planted a low box hedge around the perimeter and there he stands looking down over the parkland, his feet surrounded by the mauve and white native violet, which has formed a thick mat through which pink tulips (fittingly named 'Sauterne') push up in the spring.

With the advent of this little figure the courtyard was off to a good start. I put a small dark green iron table there, with two matching chairs, but it still looked rather bare – too much brick and not enough greenery. I had brought with me from Victoria three outsized brown ceramic pots – excellent pots that stand almost a metre high. We placed them in strategic positions in the courtyard. Now I was faced with the problem of what to grow in them.

Five or six years ago I visited Levens Hall in Cumbria, in northern England. The garden is totally dominated by its topiary. I was fascinated. From the pamphlet given me at the entrance I learnt that most of it was established about 300 years ago, towards the end of the seventeenth century. Some of the topiary was by now very large – huge animals and birds, an enormous corkscrew (very difficult to do), spirals and obelisks. The beds were all surrounded by low box hedges, and most of the topiary was yew. I was there in the spring and the beds enclosed by the box hedges were thickly planted with tulips, all of them white. Until that day I hadn't been entirely sure that I liked topiary. Levens Hall convinced me that I do.

When we got home to Erinvale I planted a couple of topiary birds. They grew well but

I don't seem to have a natural gift for shaping them. Under my inexpert hands they soon more closely resembled squirrels. The English gardener Mary Keen in her delightful book *The Glory of the English Garden* advises that 'the trick is to follow the shape of the bush. If it looks like a chicken it will never make a peacock.'

In the little Tasmanian town of Evandale there is a topiary nursery on the banks of the South Esk River. It is surrounded by a sophisticated garden. Many nurseries have disappointing gardens – I suspect the owners simply haven't the time to tend both nursery and garden – but this one is the reverse. A walk around Tim Barbour's nursery, Topiarius, and its garden shows exactly what can be achieved with standards, with topiary, with espaliering.

It is not a big garden but Tim believes in massed planting. Various clipped ivies are used as underplantings for groves of silver birches, as well as for small beds enclosed by low box hedges. Espaliered apple trees are a joy for months, both in flower and in fruit. Standard roses grow on either side of stone-flagged paths. And in the nursery I found many of the things that had so delighted me at Levens Hall: chickens and peacocks and swans (birds seem to lend themselves to topiary), obelisks and pyramids and balls. Tim uses not only box but also lonicera, privet, escallonia, cotoneaster and even grapevines for his topiary work. There are also espaliered apple trees and standardised fuchsias – anything that can be successfully trained and shaped. Some of the pieces on view have taken years to form. Growing topiary is a slow process. Some are in pots. Most are in the ground and Tim undertakes to dig up what you want.

I found them all irresistible. I stayed an hour or so choosing and rejecting and changing my mind, talking, drinking coffee, tasting the gourmet sauces his wife, Julie, makes,

---

Following pages left From Topiarius, Tim Barbour's topiary nursery,
I chose the plants I wanted for the shady courtyard. *Following
pages right* The espaliered apple walk at Topiarius is as lovely in
autumn when the apples ripen as it is when covered in spring blossom.
At the end of the walk are two of the crab apple *Malus aldenhamensis*
and in the central section multi-grafted apples.

and chatting with the very friendly golden labrador. In the end I left having arranged that Tim would deliver to Forest Hall three magnificent well-formed birds, two of privet and one of box, to go in the three big brown pots; two little standardised cotoneasters, with plaited stems, to go in smaller pots (not yet acquired) on either side of the french doors opening from the sitting room; and two tiny pink standard fuchsias to go under the kitchen window, on either side of a dark green iron birdbath. With these all finally planted (with slow-release fertiliser in the bottom of each pot) our shady courtyard was transformed. From being something of a Cinderella it has become one of the more interesting features of the garden. As for the shaping of the topiary: John turned out to be a natural. He has a steady hand and a straight eye and in his care the birds, unlike my earlier attempts at Erinvale, are still unmistakably birds.

Later I found another pot to stand at the bottom of the new downpipe coming from one of the upstairs bathrooms. (Old houses like Forest Hall didn't have plastic downpipes. Neither for that matter did they have upstairs bathrooms.) I wound green plastic lattice round the pipe and planted the pot with *Jasminum polyanthum*. In a very short time the jasmine had reached the top, effectively disguising both the downpipe and the plastic lattice, its fragrant pink and white flowers scenting the courtyard on warm evenings.

The front garden

It was well over a year before I seriously tackled the front garden. Mainly because it was, quite simply, too hard. As is the case with many old Tasmanian gardens, the area in front of the house was parkland. Here were some of the best of the trees.

There is a magnificent close relative of the sequoia, *Sequoiadendron giganteum*. Until I came upon Thomas Packenham's book *Meetings with Remarkable Trees* I had not known that the name came from Sequoya, the American Indian who invented an alphabet for the native American languages. I don't know that such scraps of information necessarily add anything to one's pleasure in the garden. And yet to me they link it to places far away and times long past.

There are two splendid cedars, which were placed symmetrically on either side of the front door but some 50 metres away from it. One has done better than the other. Both bear picturesque cones that look like little semi-single roses and are avidly collected and treasured by visiting grandchildren.

The larch. One of the joys of the garden. Here it has all the space it needs, its graceful drooping branches not crowded by other, lesser trees. I love Hugh Johnson's description of them in his *Encyclopaedia of Trees*: 'we love the larches for being different; for flushing feathery green in April; for glowing gold in November; even for spending the winter as a tangle of bare black rigging'. They are long lived. Packenham tells of three larches in Ultental in the Alps that are 2200 years old.

In a narrow bed along the top of the retaining wall in front of the house I planted a collection of China roses, which give colour for many months. 'Old Blush' is here and 'Slater's Crimson China' and the odd, green 'Viridiflora'. At the base of the wall our four-wheeled motorbike stands ready for action.

As children we listened avidly as my mother read us Longfellow's tales of Hiawatha. Seeking wood to build his canoe, he cried:

'Give me of your roots, O Tamarack,
Of your fibrous roots, O larch tree,
My canoe to bind together
That the water may not enter
That the river may not wet me.'

Growing up in sunny Queensland I don't suppose I had ever seen a larch tree but the lines remained with me.

Along the drive are the oaks and aspens that had so delighted us on our first sight of Forest Hall. They are now a great age and apt to drop branches in a high wind. And near the top of the drive is one of the most statuesque lindens I have seen: *Tilia petiolaris*, the weeping silver lime. It towers over the sweet chestnut beside it and the trunk of a deceased monkey puzzle on the opposite side. The linden's flowers scent the garden in spring and its bare branches form a delicate tracery against the winter sky.

There is a little cluster of *Robinia pseudoacacia*. Robinias are named for John Tradescant's friend Jean Robin, curator of the Paris Jardin des Plantes. Ours are old and misshapen but their rough, furrowed, greyish bark is attractive still. The suckers they send up in myriads are not. Nor are their thorns.

And of course there are the hollies – which seed themselves in hundreds even in the paddocks – and the laurels, which do likewise. And the cordylines that I so dislike. I took two out but left two along the front fence in deference to Forest Hall's history.

There is one comparatively young conifer – 50 years old perhaps – and at its feet a small planting of deep blue muscari, the only ones in the front garden and densely packed now. Locals tell us a child is buried there. Certainly the planting is in the shape of a small grave. There must have been many such in the harsh days of early settlement.

We have planted trees in our turn in the hope that in this gentle climate they will flourish and replace the old ones when their time has expired, and in the hope that we too might leave a legacy for our successors as William Bonnily has done for us.

Very early, before we had even moved in, we planted two tulip trees (*Liriodendron tulipifera*), from North America, chosen for their golden leaves in autumn and their strange greenish yellow, tulip-shaped flowers in summer. And two strawberry trees, because they are evergreen: *Arbutus* × *andrachnoides* and *A. glandulosa* for their rich cinnamon-coloured bark. And another tilia in case we should lose the splendid one on the drive. Also one *Sorbus aria* 'Lutescens' – the whitebeam, so called because the leaves in spring are silvery white. It was my favourite among the dozen or so sorbus we had grown in Victoria. I had not realised that the insatiable pear slug, which feasts on pears, quinces and prunus and makes its home in the hawthorn hedges that surround the garden, would regard this as a special delicacy. And one Kashmir cypress (*Cupressus cashmeriana*) for its delightful blue-green foliage and weeping habit, and one *Cedrus atlantica glauca* for much the same reason, although it will ultimately grow into a far bigger tree. This was a fine beginning and we have continued to plant trees over the ensuing years.

Down towards the front gate, beneath an overhanging aspen, was a small pond. A very small pond. Really just an apology for a pond. It dried up completely at the merest suggestion of hot weather. But it was situated just where a pond ought to be, at the lowest point in the garden. And I did want ornamental water within the garden itself. If it was deeper perhaps it would hold water for longer.

The farmer next door volunteered the names of a couple of excavators – this was too big a job for Philip's machine – and I selected one at random. That evening, some time after 7, there was a great commotion on the drive, with much agitated barking from Rose, our new young red heeler, and deep rumbling growls from old Joh. When I went out to investigate I found a gleaming Harley-Davidson parked there. Its bearded and bespectacled owner was trying in vain to make friends with Rose. As I came out he turned his attention from Rose to me, greeted me with a charming smile and asked if I would like to come for a spin. I think he felt spurned – and I felt cowardly – when I declined.

He examined the pond carefully, assured me he could make it hold water, said he would be back in the morning, jumped on the Harley-Davidson and roared away up the highway at top speed. I wondered whether I would ever see him again.

But at 6 o'clock the next morning (it was winter and still dark) I heard the sound of a

At the foot of a conifer in the
front garden is a dense planting
of muscari – the only ones in this
part of the garden. It reputedly
marks the grave of a small child.

motor, looked out of my bedroom window and saw him working away in the pond under lights.

He was moderately successful. The pool holds water for most of the year. He positioned two flat rocks at the edge and on one of them I put a much-loved piece of sculpture, which I had brought with me from Victoria – a long-haired girl looking down into the water, her hands clasping her knees. I had bought it years ago at an exhibition in Sydney. The model was my daughter's closest friend. This year I shall plant waterlilies in the pond.

At some time one of the gates of the original semicircular drive had been closed off, leaving only one. We were refused permission to reinstate the other because of the increased volume of traffic on the Bass Highway.

The land slopes gently up from the road and the house stands a metre or so above the level of the lawn. A fine sandstone wall runs the full width of the house, 4 metres beyond the veranda. But although the drive had obviously swept across the front of the house, and the front door is one of the most gracious and stately I have seen in Tasmania, there is no flight of grand front steps. Access is from steps to the north-west of the veranda. I asked all the one-time residents who visited us, including the now 100-year-old Molly Pedley, but none of them recalled there ever having been front steps.

A copy of a watercolour painted about 1940 showed a hedge across the front of the house – box? Privet? It was hard to tell. But it quite hid the lovely old retaining wall. I was grateful to whichever subsequent owner had removed it. In its place I planted 600 of the scarlet tulips I had bought from Judith Bowden at Bothwell. Once there had been a balustrade of some sort along the top of the wall for there are still 20-centimetre high metal posts at regular intervals.

I think the absence of front steps was partly responsible for my delay in tackling the front garden. I could not decide whether to have steps constructed from our plentiful stone or to leave it as it was, with only the decidedly uninspiring steps at the side. Then there was the question of the veranda. Had it always been there? Or was it a later addition? I leant towards the latter theory for the first-floor french doors above the front entrance were unfunctional. Had they once opened? Had there perhaps originally been a portico? Had the veranda been added as protection from the weather, given that the house faces south-west?

Since I could find no answer to any of these questions it seemed best to wait. Perhaps we might one day have a visitor who could answer them.

I left the parkland as it was, with its giant trees and its carpets of bulbs, and concentrated on the narrow strip of garden between the veranda and the stone retaining wall. Someone had made a garden – perhaps a metre wide and 30 metres long, at the top of the wall. It was planted with two odd 1940s Hybrid Teas, orange marigolds and red and mauve gladioli. It took many hours of digging and several doses of Fusilade to remove the couch grass that had its roots far down in the stone wall.

I decided to devote this bed mainly to China roses. I wanted things that would not grow too tall and detract from the simple dignity of the house. I had planted the first of the four 'stud Chinas', 'Parks' Yellow Tea-scented China', in the blacksmith's garden because the colour was right, but I still had to find the right place for the other three. Graham Thomas wrote of the China rose that its influence in rose breeding over nearly 200 years 'has been so great, so overwhelming and so potent that it is difficult to see where we should have been without it'.

The best known of the four is 'Old Blush', which I had already planted in the 'herb garden'. It had come so early to Tasmania that I feel sure it would have been available to William Bonnily – or perhaps I should say to Sarah Bonnily for it was probably she who made the garden. I would love to make a hedge of 'Old Blush' one day but meanwhile I have planted two in the garden on top of the wall.

Then there is 'Slater's Crimson China', which is responsible for the clear, bright crimson colouring in many modern roses. It was introduced from China in 1792 and bears its dear little cupped red roses for as long as 'Old Blush' bears its pink ones. I saw it first years ago (in its climbing form) growing along the front of Alister Clark's house at Glenara in company with the yellow Banksia rose (*R. banksiae* 'Lutea') and a blue wisteria. I planted two of the bush form initially and was given a cutting-grown one later, which I added to this same bed.

The fourth of the stud Chinas is 'Hume's Blush Tea-scented China', reputed to be a cross between *R. chinensis* and *R. gigantea* and regarded as delicate. It played an important role in the breeding of the early Tea roses so I wanted to include it. As it grows far too tall

Joh never fails to have a drink from the pond when he goes down with Bill each morning to collect the papers. *Opposite above* Steps at the side of the house lead to the veranda. They are overhung with 'Dorothy Perkins' and *Fuchsia magellanica*. *Opposite below* 'Old Blush' is one of the longest-flowering roses in the garden. It is found in many churchyards and old gardens, including the garden at Port Arthur.

for this bed on top of the wall, I found a protected spot for it round the back, in the corner where the chimney of the bread oven juts out, and gave it a tripod as support. There is some lingering doubt whether the rose we call 'Hume's Blush Tea-scented China' is the true one but until there is proof to the contrary I shall continue to treasure it. Its large, full, deliciously fragrant, blush white flowers fully justify its place in the garden as long as we acknowledge that it is historically suspect. The Chinas form the basis of the narrow bed on top of the wall. To these I added 'Hermosa', which is very similar to 'Old Blush', and 'Cramoisi Supérieur', which is the same clear crimson as 'Slater's Crimson'. Both of these seldom reach more than a metre.

At the north-west end of the bed was a huge ungainly bush of *Berberis darwinii*. This evergreen shrub seems to have enjoyed considerable popularity among Victorian garden-ers. It comes from Chile and the Argentine and bears mustard-yellow flowers in late winter and spring just in time to clash horribly with the fresh spring gold of the daffodils. It had to go. Its extremely prickly leaves made this a painful task but eventually we triumphed, and in its place – after the addition of much good topsoil – I planted the freakish 'Viridiflora', the green rose. Gardeners have found it interesting rather than beautiful but sophisticated flower arrangers love it. Graham Thomas cannot be numbered among its admirers. He says that 'on opening it becomes loose and tawdry splashed with brown and cannot be called beautiful'. Jack Harkness describes it as 'an engaging monstrosity'. Tucked away at the end of my bed it attracts little attention, especially as the exquisite 'Cloth of Gold' planted by the side steps is threatening to creep round the corner and overwhelm it entirely.

The drive from Launceston to Elizabeth Town takes us through the little village of Hagley, remarkable for nothing except its shocking-pink pub. On the front fence of an undistinguished weatherboard cottage I noticed a small pink rose that seemed to be con-stantly in flower. It stood entirely alone, the only living thing in a gravelled front yard. After admiring it for well over two years I resolved one day to ask if I might have a cutting. The owner proved to be a delightful white-haired old lady ('Probably about our age,' Bill said) who had lived there for over fifty years, during which time this rose had been a constant joy to her. It received no attention for she was no gardener but she loved the little fully double, pink flowers and was intrigued by the fact that there were often two colours on the bush because the flowers deepened as they aged. (This is typical of China roses.) She gladly gave me cuttings, only one of which took. I think it *may* be 'Le Vésuve', bred by Laffay in 1825. The 'Le Vésuve' I had planted earlier had not yet produced a flower so I make this claim with no great conviction, but what is certain is that the cutting has made a charming rose and merits its place in any garden. (In the end I had to move it, although I love it dearly, because it grew much too tall – and wide – for this bed of small roses.)

Near where I had planted it I added the early polyantha rose 'Anna Maria de Montravel', which bears minute, violet-scented, double white flowers and seldom grows over 30 centimetres. Also 'Louis XIV', deepest darkest red, with a scent to match and seldom reaching 60 centimetres. And 'L'Ouche' (named after a river in France), which bears its charming pink flowers in great abundance. It grows somewhat taller than the others, sometimes to a metre, so was relegated to the end of the bed beside a hedge of the little red *Fuchsia magellanica*, again from Chile and the Argentine and sometimes called ladies' eardrops. It is found in many old gardens and must have been in this one for a very long time as it was so dense that it was two years before I found the small flight of stone steps that leads down beneath it to the shrubbery.

Several of what Swane's nursery in Sydney call Cottage Garden Roses were added to this bed of historically significant roses. Named for English counties, some were bred in Denmark, some in Germany. They form low-growing shrubs that bear clusters of charming small double roses over a very long period. 'Kent' is purest white, 'Devon' palest apricot, 'Surrey' pale pink. Although of very recent origin ('Kent' was bred in 1988) they are perfect companions for the little China roses. On alternate veranda posts I planted, after long deliberation, the deep pink, almost crimson, 'Fellemberg'. Sometimes classed as a China and sometimes as a Noisette, it seldom grows much over 2 metres and bears its flowers in great clusters over a very long period. Wonderfully regal, deep red peonies came up all through the bed, and dark purple irises planted goodness knows how long ago – long before the gaudy Hybrid Teas, the orange marigolds and the dreary gladioli I had removed.

On alternate front veranda posts
is 'Fellemberg' (seen in detail
above), sometimes classed as
a China rose, sometimes as a
Noisette. It flowers long and
generously. In the foreground
is 'Carabella'. The little white
rose on top of the wall is 'Kent',
which sits comfortably with
the China roses.

The red and grey garden

IN THE SUMMER OF 1999 I had a visit from Lynette Cooke, a friend who is an experienced and innovative gardener. The red roses in Willy's extended garden were doing well. Behind them the ground sloped gradually up to the fence that marked the end of the cultivated garden. Far up in the paddocks beyond was the line of grand old Magna Cartas, their furrowed trunks forming an impenetrable barrier and providing a dense backdrop to the garden. I had done nothing to the area between the red roses and the fence. It was still entirely given over to blackberry and bracken and great outcrops of stone.

Lynette had recently had a holiday in Greece and she had come home treasuring a mental picture of blue skies and sunshine and olive groves terraced down to the sea. We certainly have the blue skies and the sunshine. And in place of the sea a range of ever-changing blue mountains. Lynette suggested planting an olive grove between the roses and the fence, with a thick underplanting of irises. Both olives and irises would revel in the open, exposed position, and the grey of the olives would be a splendid contrast to the dark green of the macrocarpas further up the hill.

It was an inspired suggestion – most of Lynette's suggestions are – and I turned it over in my mind continually in the next couple of weeks. I even paced it out and calculated how many olives I would have room for and where I could plant the irises. But groves of olives – groves of any kind of orchard tree – really need to be planted in straight lines to achieve the desired effect and straight lines were an impossibility here because of the irregular shape and placing of the rocks.

I recalled a visit I had made some years ago to the rose garden at Castle Howard in northern England – one of the loveliest rose gardens I have seen. One of the main features of the garden was the planting of weeping silver pears (*Pyrus salicifolia* 'Pendula'). They were distributed through the garden as backdrops for the roses. They are by nature unruly, ill-disciplined trees, their pendulous branches twisting and curving in all directions. They would look incongruous planted in straight lines. I could plant them where they fitted best among the rocks. And I would still have the contrast of silver grey against the dark green.

So I ordered eight, which I would plant in autumn. I love autumn planting. Things get a chance to settle in while the ground is still warm. Then in spring they are ready to shoot away.

While we were waiting for the trees, John and I did the preparatory work of cleaning up the slope. Gradually we got rid of the blackberry and the thistles and the bracken and in the process uncovered more rock than I had thought was there: great grey lichen-covered boulders.

I decided to add three *Elaeagnus angustifolia*. This beautiful little tree has foliage as silver as that of the pears. I first saw it at some distance on the far side of Helen Dillon's exquisite small garden in Dublin and mistook it for a silver pear. At the foot of one of mine I planted the deep purple-blue clematis 'General Sikorski'.

Then to echo the red of Willy's garden I included three *Cotinus coggygria*: two 'Royal Purple' and one 'Grace'. Cotinus has fascinating dark purple-red foliage. The small tree received the nickname 'smoke bush' because the fluffy heads of the minute flowers look like puffs of smoke.

For autumn colour it is hard to beat *Euonymus alatus*, the winged spindle bush. I planted two of the variety known as 'Red Chief', which is so vivid the whole bush seems to be on fire. The seeds are formed in capsules that burst open and reveal bright red and orange seeds. There was a huge holly already in place on the north-west border, bearing scarlet berries in winter. On the south-east boundary is an ash that turns gold in autumn. I now had trees enough. But that Christmas we had a live Christmas tree as the grandchildren were visiting. After they had gone home we planted the tree in this part of the garden. It is a spruce from western China – *Picea likiangensis* var. *purpurea*. I love the blue-grey foliage, and in addition it bears charming little purple cones.

The whole area of Willy's garden was gradually filled with red and grey plants. The dark green of the macrocarpas formed a splendid background, framed by the holly on the left and an ash tree on the right.

It was at this point that I was given a bucketful of pieces of a dark red gallica rose by a friend who had sold her house, and the lovely garden around it, and could not bear to leave this beauty behind. It is something of a mystery rose: 'Assemblage des Beautés'. It was released in France in 1823 but its parentage is unknown. It is strongly fragrant, a dark red verging on purple, very full and quartered, with a button eye. I felt sure that it would send out suckers if grown on its own roots. Most gallicas do. I put fifteen cuttings in pots and twelve of them struck. I decided to treat them as a hedge and planted them along the south-east fence of the grey and red garden. It will not matter how much they sucker here. I remembered the dense, impenetrable banks of gallicas at Tanglewood, Maria Fawcett's intriguing garden in Melbourne. In time mine might rival these. I underplanted them with *Artemisia absinthium* 'Lambrook Silver' (Margery Fish again!), and round the weeping silver pear that marked the end of the hedge I planted some dark red dahlias I had found coming up unexpectedly in the shrubbery.

Against two of the bigger rocks I planted cardoons (*Cynara cardunculus*). Their huge sculptured silver-grey leaves and purple thistlelike flowers tower up over head height. In their second year they started to self-seed – not enough to be a nuisance, just enough to provide replacements. I am told the leafy stalks are edible and a worthy addition to summer salads, but I haven't been able to persuade myself to try them.

Roses can't be relied upon to come true from seed and most of the seedlings that come up in a big garden are not worth keeping. But years ago when I was at Bleak House a really worthwhile seedling came up in a bed of Rugosas. I think one of the parents was the purple 'Roseraie de l'Haÿ'. I'm not sure what the other one was. The tiny plant grew and prospered – largely because I didn't have time to weed the bed – otherwise it would have gone down the crimson path to the bonfire like most of my seedlings. When it put out its first tentative flower I was delighted. It was large and scented, a softer colour than 'Roseraie de l'Haÿ' and nearly as double. I was even more delighted when the little plant flowered again in autumn.

So when I moved from Bleak House to Erinvale I dug it up and took it with me. I planted it on a bank of Rugosas, with lilac-blue *Campanula persicifolia* and a handful of bulbs of *Tulbaghia violacea*, the so-called society garlic. The latter sends up its small mauve flowers over a long period and seems to need no attention. It is reputed by English writers to be an effective mole deterrent. I haven't noticed that our rabbits or bandicoots are in the least put off by it.

When we were planning our move to Tasmania this seedling rose was one of a very few I wanted to take with me. As it was a chance seedling I would never be able to get it again. So I asked John Nieuwesteeg to bud a couple of plants for me. He does it so much better than I do. In our first winter down here I put in a big rose order. I hoped John might remember my seedling rose. Of course he had. But he sent me not the two or three I had asked for but a bundle of twenty-two beautiful strong healthy plants – enough to make a hedge. And Rugosas make the best hedges of all. So I made a bed along the north-east boundary of the red and grey garden and settled them in.

They have made an excellent hedge. It is now 1.5 metres tall and so dense that even the heelers don't push their way through. When he took the budwood John had asked me to give it a distinguishing name, so I had called it 'Niree Hunter' after my mother. She was not a gardener but she loved flowers and all things beautiful. She had a real gift for arranging flowers and I remember that whenever we had guests coming (which was often because she was so hospitable) her first task was to do great bowls of flowers – preferably roses, her favourite being 'my lovely "Mme Abel Chatenay"'. So my seedling rose goes by her name and would without doubt have been a joy to her. The name 'Niree Hunter' confuses everybody. The rose has been referred to as 'Marie Hunter', 'Irene Hunter', 'Myra Hunter', for most people have never heard the name Niree. Small wonder. It is a part of the family's (rather eccentric) Tasmanian heritage.

My great-grandfather John Woodcock Graves was a solicitor in Hobart, an irascible individualist who none the less took a genuine interest in the well-being of the last of the island's Aborigines, even (according to family history) having Truganini, the lone survivor of the indigenous people, to live on his property for a time.

John Graves wanted a son and his poor wife produced nothing but daughters. First came Jean, then May. By the time the third one arrived his interest in the Aborigines had been kindled and he called her Mathinna (a watering place in the local dialect). My grandmother was next. She was named MiMi (a dwelling place). The arrival of the fifth daughter

The great grey sculptured leaves of the cardoons (*Cynara cardunculus*) dominate the red and grey garden in summer. The seed heads are striking in winter. *Opposite above* The spinosissima hybrid 'Single Cherry' is planted alternately with *Lavendula stoechas*. Behind is the grey foliage of one of the young weeping silver pears (*Pyrus salicifolia* 'Pendula'). *Opposite below* The hedge of red hawthorns (*Crataegus laevigata* 'Paul's Scarlet'), intermingled with rambling roses, that I planted to hide the work area.

was almost more than John Woodcock could bear. He strode into the bedroom where poor little Grannie still lay in bed, cast a contemptuous look at the new arrival and shouted, 'You're Truganini!' And Truganini she was.

I remember her well – a tall spare dictatorial intimidating figure who lived when I was a child in a fine old house on the banks of the Brisbane River. We were taken to stay there each time we went to Brisbane to visit the dentist. I never knew which terrified me the more – the dentist (in the days before local anaesthetics) or Aunt Truca as she was called in the family.

My grandmother's name, MiMi, was handed on to me as a second name – to my intense chagrin. I hated having a name no one had heard of and used it as little as possible. And yet I think we would have had a great deal in common. I am quite sure it was from her that I inherited my passion for gardening. From the age of 18, as the result of an attack of measles, she was profoundly deaf. She died before I was born and the only portrait I have of her shows her, dressed in a long white gown, her white hair softly curling, sitting in a wicker chair in the garden at a table covered in flowers, a single rose held between her fingers.

And that is how my mother remembered her – always in the garden, communicating, perhaps because of her deafness, more easily with plants than with people. Possibly she inherited something of her eccentric father's concern for the Aborigines for she called her only daughter Niree – a good woman.

Below the hedge of 'Niree Hunter' a low bank slopes down to a path. On this bank I planted the silver-grey *Cupressus macrocarpa* 'Greenstead Magnificent', which is prostrate and forms a thick mat. And I took my plants of spinosissima 'Single Cherry' out of the pots I had put them in for safe keeping and used them to line the other side of the path, interspersed with the dark violet-purple *Lavandula stoechas* – lavender is essential in a garden. According to ancient legend it 'breathes forth the breath of paradise'.

The north-west boundary of the red and grey garden is adjacent to the work area across the drive. Every garden needs a work area – in our case an area for the clothesline, the compost bins, a wood heap to serve the open fires we have in the winter. And we always seem to have a pile of tan bark and gravel and sand left over from the last job and saved for the next. So this area, which is not a thing of beauty, had to be fenced off.

Years ago I helped a friend in the country make a hedge round a big rambling garden. She already had dozens of hawthorn plants and wanted to use them. I had a multitude of potted plants of the rambling rose 'Albertine'. So we planted them together. The rose pushed its way up through the hawthorn and the effect was stunning. Many of the hawthorn hedges in Tasmania are interspersed with the little pink and white dog rose (*R. canina*) and white daisies, bringing back memories of motoring down English country lanes.

I decided to use the red hawthorn *Crataegus laevigata* 'Paul's Scarlet', planted 1.5 metres apart, to hide the work area. I needed fourteen. They are hardy and fast growing and enchanting in flower. I had plenty of plants of 'Albertine'. I always have plenty of plants of 'Albertine'. It is such a treasure of a rose that I can never resist putting in cuttings when I prune it after flowering. And they all take. But this time in the hawthorn hedge I used several different roses.

I had just acquired a plant of 'Lady Medallist'. Released in 1912 this was Alister Clark's first great success. He named it for one of his racehorses – also a success. I had looked for it for years unsuccessfully. None of the rose nurseries stocked it. Most of them had never heard of it. Then unexpectedly it turned up a few years ago in a neglected garden in Western Australia. It is a vigorous climber. So I planted it between two of the red hawthorns and trained the long shoots horizontally. The first large, almost voluptuous, mid-pink flowers appeared in early spring.

Another Alister Clark rose I had not previously grown is 'Cicely O'Rorke'. It is also a vigorous climber. The semi-single flowers are pink, but unlike those of 'Lady Medallist' they are borne recurrently. It was named for a niece of Alister's wife, Edith, and fittingly she was a talented painter of watercolours. I planted it between the next two hawthorns.

Then came 'Mme Alice Garnier'. I had struck cuttings from the two I had planted on one of the pergolas so I used them here. It is an odd little rose, its pale pink flowers quilled and quartered and rather confused. Its thorns are vicious. It grows quickly and flowers recurrently. Graham Thomas describes its scent as being 'reminiscent of green apples'. This rose is equally happy used as a climber or a groundcover. I planted it at Erinvale to cover a steep bank. It was not a wise choice. It was happy to trail down over the bank but it

In no time 'Albertine' blocked the gate that led through to the drying and work area from the former kitchen garden.

was so thorny that weeding under it was akin to torture. However, scrambling up among the hawthorns it is very effective and the pale pink blooms are a lovely contrast to the cherry red of the hawthorns.

The pale pink and white rose from China that was used extensively in earlier years as an understock in Australia under the name 'indica major' is found in many old gardens, in churchyards and even by the roadside, where the understock has taken over from the scion. It blooms early and briefly but at its peak it is a picture. Feeling that no collection of old roses would be complete without it I used three among the hawthorns.

And for contrast and because it looks stunning with the pink of the roses and the red of the hawthorns, I included the deep purple 'Veilchenblau'. Then I filled the remaining spaces with 'Albertine'.

Even in its second year this hedge was beginning to make an effective screen. Now it almost hides the compost bins. The clothesline, being taller, will take another year to disappear. Eventually I think the hedge will be a striking feature of the garden.

My grandmother MiMi Graves.

Then
the irises

WITH THE TREES planted in the red and grey garden and the boundaries defined I turned to Lynette's second suggestion – irises. A sea of irises she had suggested – and planted on their own in great drifts, not in company with other perennials.

There were irises in the garden when we came. However, the *I. unguicularis* we had found in thick clumps in the shrubbery and under the big laurel on the drive didn't flower that first year. They were too congested. I divided them and replanted them. They didn't flower the next season either. I think they hate being disturbed. But in our third year we were rewarded by a sea of lilac-blue flowers in late winter and early spring. They benefit from having the foliage cut back so that it doesn't obscure the flowers.

The next iris to flower for us was *I. × xiphium* – soft lilac blue and yellow. The bulbs multiply quickly and their flowering period often coincides with that of the tulips. I planted them with the yellow tulip 'Big Smile' around the rose arbour we built last year, where I had originally put blue Dutch irises – these had been something of a disappointment because they bloomed much later than the tulips, so my vision of blue and gold had failed to materialise.

In a damp spot near a rivulet that runs down beside the drive, there were big colonies of *I. pseudacorus*, which flowered over a long period and didn't in the least object to being mown down when they had finished. It was from these that we had taken the *I. pseudacorus* we planted in the lake paddock. The tall white *I. ochroleuca* (synonymous with *I. orientalis*)

In October the blue and mauve irises, growing among the boulders and under the silver pears and euonymus, take over the red and grey garden.

came up in various places and gradually we moved them all to the one spot near the lake, where they continue to flower with no attention whatsoever.

There were some tall bearded irises in the beds near the house, but they were in drab old-fashioned colours – a rather dreary purple and what Gertrude Jekyll referred to as 'malignant magenta'. They gave the impression of having been here for very many years and having lost interest in putting on much of a spring show. I hate throwing away plants but bit by bit these old irises were dug out and more interesting things took their place.

It was tall bearded irises that I wanted in the red and grey garden. The position was perfect for them – open and sunny and well drained – and they would benefit from the occasional handful of lime given to the roses. Their tall, swordlike leaves are a wonderful foil for roses. They require little care, but they benefit from being divided every four or five years, when the old rhizomes should be discarded and the new young shoots encouraged. What makes them invaluable in a rose garden is that they flower after the spring bulbs have put on their magnificent display and before the first of the roses. This is a period that can be something of a let-down. The irises ensure that it will be anything but.

I planted them at the base of the silver pears: blues – every shade of blue – and purples and white. And all around the big rocks: yellows and cream and eau-de-nil and every combination of these. And under the cardoons: pinks and ruby red. It doesn't matter that this is intended to be a red and grey garden for at the time the irises flower there is scarcely a rose to be seen, not a sedum or a penstemon. For the month of October this garden is all the colours of the rainbow. The daffodils at Forest Hall are a glory in September, in November the roses steal the show completely, but October belongs to the irises – with just a little help from the tulips.

I go through the red and grey garden every morning in October with a bucket and secateurs, snipping off the dead heads of the irises so that nothing will mar the display. I don't remember their names. While I can confidently tell visitors the name of every rose in the garden, I am ashamed to say I remember almost none of the iris names. This is not because I value them any less. They must be among the most beautiful, the most stately, the most regal of garden plants.

Gradually I am adding to the collection. The *I. kaempferi* and *I. sibirica* I planted near the lake are steadily increasing. I put a few of the tiny *I. cristata* in the shrubbery for they need gentler conditions. I was given several *I. japonica*, with their tall leaves and palest blue, ruffled flowers. These I put in the shrubbery also as they don't care for too much harsh sun. From Norgate's I got several varieties of *I. innominata* – pale pink, deep blue and sunshiny yellow. I put them under some shrub roses for they don't grow tall. Next winter I shall divide the clumps and expect to have at least three times as many.

I visited a garden that specialises in small bulbs and was bowled over by a carpet of tiny *I. reticulata* 'Harmony' – sky blue, with royal-blue falls. I planted some in a little stone trough outside the kitchen door. I was frightened to put them in the garden. They are so small and so low growing I could miss seeing them in their hour of glory.

I have bought a copy of Brian Mathew's scholarly book *The Iris*, but it has served principally to confuse me. Like everything else in the plant world, the iris family is incredibly complex. So I shall go on collecting and loving and admiring them, and not worry too much if their infinite variety continues to perplex me.

Taking in the oak paddock

THE LEFT-HAND SIDE of the drive up to the house is lined with hawthorns. Not a hedge, just ancient hawthorns closely planted and allowed to grow into trees. I think they have never been clipped or pruned. Unlike the hawthorn hedges along the country roads in Tasmania, which are mostly white, these trees are pale apple-blossom pink and cherry red as well.

It is between these hawthorns and the drive that a little ditch in wet weather turns into the rivulet where the *Iris pseudacorus* grow. It tumbles down between mossy boulders and is fed from a spring far up in the paddock. At the gate it flows under the highway, eventually joining the Rubicon River – a tiny stream at this stage, not much more than a trickle, but assuming quite imposing proportions as it nears the sea. Our little rivulet, a rushing torrent during rainy periods, runs for weeks after the rain has stopped.

Behind the hawthorns was a rough-hewn post-and-rail fence that announced that this was the end of the garden. From here onward the cattle were allowed to graze. But looking at the trees in the paddock just beyond the fence I felt sure this had not always been so. There were no fewer than five venerable oaks in this paddock. And an elm, a larch,

Opposite After heavy rain the little rivulet beside the front drive turns into a rushing torrent, tumbling down over mossy boulders under the hawthorns bordering the oak paddock.

an ash, a chestnut and a blackwood. It must originally have been part of the garden. However, it was so overgrown with blackberry, gorse and bracken that trying to walk through it was a dangerous and painful exercise. Not to mention the boulders that lay hidden beneath the undergrowth and were a trap for unwary feet.

It was the fly agaric (*Amanita muscaria*) that made me decide to remove the fence and bring this intriguing wild piece of woodland into the garden. They came up in their hundreds in the autumn – those fascinating orange-scarlet toadstools with white spots that we all remember from childhood stories of elves and fairies – another welcome surprise in our first year at Forest Hall. They appeared overnight, under the oak trees. These are the conditions they love, thriving in the thick mulch created by the fallen oak leaves. They are, like so many beautiful fungi, deadly poisonous. But animals seem to know this and leave them strictly alone.

We removed the old wooden fence – not without difficulty for in some places it was actually nailed to the hawthorns – and added this acre to the garden. I didn't want to remove or clip the hawthorn hedge. It is a picture in spring. But it was essential to connect the oak paddock to the garden and make it appear an integral part of it. So I cut two arches in the hedge and built two little bridges over the rivulet, so that now leafy paths lead through into the oak paddock. We used old timber for the bridges, timber we found in the stables. New timber would have been out of place.

Along the banks of the rivulet, under the hawthorns, I decided to plant hellebores and pulmonarias, aquilegias and ajugas. I wanted a dense carpet in this deeply shaded area. My first choice was hellebores. They must be among the most rewarding of garden plants. While the days are still short and cold and snow is still lying on the Tiers they burst into flower. And they seed so generously that where you start with half a dozen within a year or two you can have hundreds.

Gardeners are generous people. I was given hellebores, not in twos and threes but by the boxful and sackload: *Helleborus corsicus*, *H. niger*, *H. orientalis*. I did not look for named varieties – although I love the one named after the home of Valerie Finnis, who was famous as a plant photographer as well as a gardener, *H. × sternii* 'Boughton Beauty'. What I really wanted was quantity. I wanted them the whole length of the drive. And

I didn't mind too much about colour, although I prefer the pure white ones, and the deep, deep reds and purples that are almost black. They will in time cross-pollinate and the range of colours will increase.

Hellebores ask for little attention. They love the leaf mulch along the bank of the rivulet and now and then I fling them a handful of fertiliser. If there is time I cut back the dead leaves and even some of the live ones because they can obscure the flowers. I laid one long line of Aquapore and turn it on occasionally when the rivulet has dried up in the middle of summer. But hellebores are without doubt among the least demanding of plants.

I specially cherish the double white one named for Betty Ranicar. Her small garden, immaculately tended and full of treasures, in the hands now of a grandson and his wife, is still a mecca for gardeners – not only from all parts of Tasmania but from the mainland as well.

To the hellebores I added many varieties of pulmonaria. These hardy woodland plants, with their spotted leaves, seem to tolerate the harshest of conditions. They mind neither frost nor dryness and, like the hellebores, self-seed, even if not quite so prolifically, and ask for little attention. At Woodbridge, in southern Tasmania, I found another of those delightful specialist nurseries for which this State is famous, which offers a wide range of pulmonarias. I started with 'Beth's Blue', which the nurseryman had got direct from Beth Chatto, 'Blue Ensign', *P. saccharata* 'Frühlingshimmel' (spring heaven) with paler blue flowers, *P. officinalis* 'Sissinghurst White' from the garden of Vita Sackville-West and *P. rubra* 'Barfield Pink'. I specially love the blues next to the green of many of the hellebores. I would grow the pulmonarias for their spotted foliage alone but their bright little flowers borne in profusion over a long period light up the shade in early spring.

All along the bank I scattered aquilegia seed. I will never forget the sight of them at Wombat Park, in Victoria, where they had naturalised under the trees for which the garden is renowned. They received no attention, were never watered or fertilised. Admittedly the rainfall is plentiful at Daylesford. They had seeded and crossed over the years and there was an amazing range of colours. I hoped mine might do the same.

The bluebells came uninvited. And I was delighted to see them. They come up each year in their thousands under the big cedars and have spread from there and formed colonies in all sorts of probable and improbable places.

The bulbs growing in the paddocks beyond the garden, under the old elm and oaks and the self-seeding hollies, seem to have no effect on the cattle, which are intuitively aware that they are toxic.

Also uninvited but not so welcome is *Arum italicum*, which had taken possession of this part of the garden (and of several other parts) long before we did. Once settled in it is hard to dislodge. Perhaps if it was a rarity and needed coaxing I might value it more. I was astonished to read Beth Chatto's description of it in *Beth Chatto's Gravel Garden*. She speaks of its dark green, glossy foliage 'vividly marbled in an exquisite pattern' with 'a plain narrow border [which] trims the wavy edge of the leaf'. Having read this and having always regarded this very vigorous spreader as a particularly obnoxious thug, I went out to have a closer look at it. I have to confess that its 'plain narrow border' had previously quite escaped my notice. But with the best will in the world, and despite the high esteem in which I hold Beth Chatto, I cannot regard it as anything but a pest. And my best efforts have failed to discourage it.

With the banks along the rivulet planted, I could now turn my attention to the oak paddock itself.

⊷━◆━⊶

The oak paddock

BEFORE WE COULD do anything else in the oak paddock, we had to get rid of the dense undergrowth. We arranged with Philip to come in and slash it. This he did very efficiently and carted the rubbish out into the paddock. The blackberry was so thick that I could see no alternative to poisoning it. So on a still, sunny day Philip came again and sprayed all the blackberry, the gorse and the bracken with Round-up. It was spring and everything bursting into growth so it was the perfect time for it. For the ensuing four weeks we stayed right away from the oak paddock. Then, when all the foliage was turning yellow, Philip slashed it again. Now we could see what we had and start planning. I hoped we hadn't disturbed the fly agaric too much.

The next step was to get rid of as many as we could of the great boulders. So Philip came once more – he was becoming indispensable – and this time he brought his excavator, which plucked the boulders out of the earth, lifted them high and piled them in big heaps. John – excited as a child in a candy shop at the prospect of more creative stonework – indicated which ones he could use for future walls and steps and the rest were carted out of the garden into the paddock beyond.

The removal of the boulders left huge holes, dangerous for pedestrians and mowers and four-wheeled bikes. The rabbits have an unfortunate habit of digging up daffodil bulbs. They don't eat them, just scatter them about. I find them whenever I walk through the daffodil paddock and I had accumulated bucketsful. I filled the holes left by the removal of the boulders with topsoil and planted daffodil bulbs in them. There was never

229

any thought of making a formal garden here. The trees and the boulders and the bulbs determined its structure. It was to be a wild garden.

It was not a place for roses. It was on the whole too shaded. But round the perimeter fence I decided to plant ramblers both to hide the fence and to cut this part of the garden off from the open paddocks and grazing stock. I used several different ramblers as I needed so many. But the hedge will be predominantly pale yellow for I planted as many as I could find of 'Goldfinch' and 'Alister Stella Gray'.

'Goldfinch' is a multiflora hybrid so almost thornless. It is vigorous but does not grow very high. The little creamy yellow flowers are borne in great clusters and fade to almost white. Graham Thomas compares their scent to that of oranges and bananas. I must confess I can't detect this.

There are very few yellow ramblers, so 'Alister Stella Gray' is doubly valuable. Whereas 'Goldfinch' flowers only in spring, this Noisette produces its charming small, perfectly shaped blooms right through to the end of autumn. I will be able to rely on it for colour long after most of the roses on the fence have ceased to flower.

A rambler I have not grown before is 'Rose-Marie Viaud'. Bred in France in 1928 it is a seedling of 'Veilchenblau' and like its parent it is almost thornless. The colour is similar: the small double flowers open a deep rosy purple and fade as they age. For a long time I have wanted to combine this deep violet with creamy yellow.

I added a couple of plants of the delightful little white 'Rambling Rector' and the totally unknown and unregistered 'Stephen Porter', given to me to try out. I am told it is a soft apricot in colour and recurrent. It has not flowered for me yet but if it doesn't blend with the soft yellows and violet it will be banished to some remote corner of the garden. It is a blessing that roses take so kindly to being moved about.

Opposite Most of the oak paddock is too shady for roses. But on an arbour we constructed I planted the comparatively shade-tolerant Bourbon 'Zéphirine Drouhin', with *Clematis armandii* 'Snow Drift' and seven cutting-grown 'Adélaide d'Orléans' roses.

On the north-east side of the oak paddock I planted a row of different buddlejas, including the lovely fountain buddleja, *B. alternifolia*, and *B. davidii* 'Black Knight' and several others given to me as cuttings. Among them I planted that outstanding rose *R. bracteata* and its striking offspring 'Mermaid' – creamy yellow and white, and lilac again.

I found in the garden great clumps of the old orange daylily *Hemerocallis fulva* 'Flore Pleno'. Its vivid orange-red colour is hard to place and I had contemplated digging it all out and putting it on the burning heap. This is something I hate to do. In fact I find it almost impossible.

The only way I really like orange in the garden is when it is combined with blue. Very fortuitously I was given at this time a sack full of agapanthus. I planted them together, the orange daylilies and the blue agapanthus, in front of the buddlejas. There was room for a couple of acanthus – it doesn't matter if they spread – and on the whole I think this randomly selected mixture has worked.

And in the end I did plant roses. Of course I did. The rustic bridges and the archways in the hawthorn hedge were all very fine. But you need to look through an archway *to* something. There must be some purpose in going through. And even a wild garden needs some element of design – paths at least. There was one sunny patch just beyond the top bridge. Here I resolved to build a rose arbour.

I was sitting one afternoon trying to design the arbour when I had a visit from the photographer Ray Joyce. I knew what I wanted but I can't draw. Ray can. He took the paper from me and in a very short space of time we had a splendid, simple design – seven stout wooden posts rising to a central peak and enclosed with wire for the roses to be attached to.

The ground slopes gently and it needed to be levelled before we could begin construction. So Philip and his excavator were summoned once again.

'Don't you think we should get rid of the widow-maker first?' he asked, pointing to the top of the old larch that was growing nearby. It was tall and emaciated, not gracefully spreading and gently weeping as a larch should be. Larches hate to be hedged about by other trees and this one was squeezed in between the hawthorns and the blackwood. Its lower branches were all gone, just a lonely topknot of leaves remaining, with one branch hanging precariously. The tree was no longer beautiful – quite the reverse. I hate felling trees but I think in this case we had no alternative. It was not a job John or Philip could tackle. Like the holly, this was a task for an expert.

We are fortunate in having in the neighbourhood a champion axeman. Matthew Gurr wins prizes for wood chopping, not only in Tasmania but also on the mainland. He inspected our larch with interest and agreed that it should go. Feeling slightly nervous about the surrounding trees and the hawthorn hedge, I asked him where it would fall. 'Just there,' he said pointing to a clear spot where it would do no damage. And it did. It took no more than a quarter of an hour.

Matthew called me over to look at the stump and showed me how he could tell from the rings that it was approximately 150 years old. From the differing widths of the rings he could also say with certainty that it had been well watered and nourished in the first ten years of its life and given little encouragement thereafter. He cut it up into lengths suitable for the open fire and carted it up to our wood heap. He had a very efficient assistant in the shape of a 6-year-old son. Country children still work with their fathers and learn their trade from an early age. I feel sure that young Luke will be a champion like his father.

With the widow-maker safely out of the way we could get to work in earnest on the rose arbour. Philip levelled the site and John built stone retaining walls where they were needed. A good deal of thought went into the clothing of the arbour. Its spot was sunnier than the rest of the oak paddock. It received perhaps four hours of sun a day. Not a lot for roses. Bourbons tolerate more shade than most, and they are almost thornless so easy to train. My first choice was my old friend 'Zéphirine Drouhin', whom Vita Sackville-West describes as 'this gentle thornless full-bosomed generous trollop of a rose'. I planted two and with them I put the gentler pink 'Kathleen Harrop', a sport of 'Zéphirine Drouhin'. It seems to be not only softer in colour but also less robust. I put it either side of the arbour doorway.

During the winter I had struck cuttings of the glorious 'Adélaide d'Orléans'. I had planted two in the herb garden at the end of the stables. One has spread and looks splendid, the deep blue-green foliage and little, round, cherry-red hips almost as entrancing as the small, double white flowers opening from pink buds. But one day the dogs thought

they scented a rabbit under the big rock the second rose was climbing on. In their frantic attempts to find it they tore the rose to pieces. I was devastated but decided to make the most of the situation, and put in seven cuttings. Every one took.

In view of the fact that both rabbits and possums frequent the oak paddock, I decided to put in all seven small plants in the hope that at least one or two might survive. Then to make assurance doubly sure I did a quick trip to Sheffield to Todd Miles's superb clematis nursery and came home with two C. *armandii* 'Snow Drift'. Possums are reputed not to like clematis. All of these have survived and by next year the arbour should be very adequately clothed. 'Kathleen Harrop' suffered in the fight for survival. The possums seemed to find her new young shoots particularly delectable. But she has not given up the struggle.

With the arbour finished, we turned our attention to the piles of selected rocks Philip had deposited near the north-west boundary. John pushed them into some sort of shape and filled the gaps and pockets with topsoil. I don't think I knew quite where I was going from there.

But by great good fortune I had a ring from John Nieuwesteeg just at this time. The Royal Botanic Gardens in Melbourne were taking out their species roses and he had the opportunity to take budwood from them. He thought I might be interested in having some of them. Most roses would not look at home in a wild garden. But species roses would. I selected five and John sent me two or three plants of each. I had never seen any of them growing.

R. blanda from North America is nearly thornless and bears small, single pink flowers, which Graham Thomas dismisses as having 'no great garden merit'. *R. beggeriana* from Asia has been compared with *R. fedtschenkoana*, with its grey foliage and small white flowers followed by dark red hips. I had grown *R. fedtschenkoana* at Bleak House and loved it, so

---

Opposite Beautiful but deadly: overnight the fly agaric (*Amanita muscaria*) appear in the oak paddock, loving the mulch provided by the oak leaves. Highly toxic for people and animals, they are never touched by the wildlife – or the dogs.

this seemed a good choice. About R. *acicularis* I could discover little except that it seems to belong to the Cinnamomea group. I don't know quite what to expect of this one. I don't even know whether it is the scent or the colour of the stems that is compared to cinnamon. R. *pendulina* comes from Europe. It is almost thornless, with reddish stems. It grows into quite a large shrub, with arching branches. The flowers are said to be attractive – light red, followed by darker red hips – and the leaves turn red and gold in autumn.

The one I am really excited about is R. *macrophylla*, which is reputed to grow 5 metres tall and 5 metres wide. It comes from the Himalayas. Many of the species roses have unexciting flowers. They are grown more for their hips and autumn colour. But this is apparently not the case with R. *macrophylla*. Graham Thomas says that the flowers 'when seen are not likely to be forgotten'. He goes further and says that 'few roses have such an elegant poise of bloom'. I can't wait!

I put two Alister Clark roses in the oak paddock. 'Courier' is a delight but it hates the frost. It bears palest pink blooms, which fade to white, on a vigorous climbing plant. It is probably a hybrid of the frost tender R. *gigantea*. It is still growing – and flowering – at Alister's home at Glenara but this is in a warm, protected valley. I had had trouble with it at Erinvale. It grew and covered itself with buds that promised great things, yet almost always we had a late frost and the buds turned brown and failed to open. But I love it, so have planted three in the shelter of the outer branches of a blackwood and so far they are doing well.

On a tree stump I planted another R. *gigantea* hybrid, which was found in a Melbourne garden. Probably it was one of Alister Clark's but we never had any proof of this. It bears large, single, palest apricot flowers not unlike those of 'Mrs Richard Turnbull' except for the colour. We called it simply 'Mrs Oswin's Gigantea' after the gardener in whose garden it was found. If it does even half as well as 'Mrs Richard Turnbull' I will be delighted.

My first introduction to old roses was a book by Gordon Edwards. On the cover was a picture of 'Rosa Mundi' growing amid a sea of foxgloves. I have never forgotten the picture and this seemed a perfect place to reproduce it.

Over a period of six weeks or so I bought a couple of punnets of foxgloves each time I visited a nursery and planted them in all the pockets of topsoil among the rocks. I hoped that in time they might naturalise as I have seen them do in many places in Tasmania.

Mown paths are ideal in a wild garden. But not in the oak paddock. The dense shade and thick leaf mulch would make growing grass difficult, if not impossible. Gravel paths would be out of place. So we used tan bark laid thickly to suppress weeds. The next autumn they were covered with fallen oak leaves and looked like genuine forest tracks.

In the front garden was that long, straight line of *Amaryllis belladonna*, the old pink naked ladies. They were so compacted that they produced very few, very reluctant flowers. I had to go out one morning just after John arrived and I had not thought what I wanted him to do. So I showed him the belladonnas, their leaves just starting to poke through, and asked him to dig them up and line one of the paths in the oak paddock with them.

When I got back a couple of hours later I sought him out and asked how he had got on with the belladonnas.

'Okay,' he said. 'I've put them in but I stopped when I got to five hundred.'

They didn't produce many flowers the following autumn – they hate being moved – but this year the buds are just starting to push through and they may even live up to the description in *Botanica*: 'a gardener's dream' giving 'a glorious display of rosy-pink lily-like flowers' – a description I would agree with, although many sophisticated gardeners would not.

Kniphofias came up in the lawn and we dug them up and systematically transplanted them to the oak paddock, where we planted them in drifts. Also sisyrinchium and species gladioli.

The oak paddock has become one of my favourite parts of the garden. The fly agaric was not disturbed and makes its dramatic appearance each autumn. As the species roses and the ramblers on the fence reach their potential it will become an increasingly private place, another secret garden, a refuge for the bandicoots and echidnas that make their homes there and the birds that nest undisturbed in the hawthorns.

At Dunedin, described in the following pages, a cypress arch some 4 metres high leads from the driveway into the garden.

Dunedin

SOME OF THE LOVELIEST plants in my garden – certainly some of the most unusual – came to me from the garden of Annabel Scott at Dunedin. A grazing property, Dunedin is just fifteen minutes' drive from Launceston. The cattle grid and unpretentious white wooden entrance posts give no indication of what is to come. The drive winds up for just on a kilometre, through paddocks of tussocky grass, dry for most of the year, and impoverished honey box trees. Black Angus cattle graze in the paddocks alongside.

The box trees, despite their appearance, yield fine honey. The beekeeper, now 94, comes every month, plunders the hives and gives the Scotts honey in exchange for the right to do so.

The first indication that you are nearing the homestead is that the drive divides, one arm going off to the right and the other going straight ahead, lined now on both sides with a magnificent cypress hedge. The drive curves round to the stables and thence under a high cypress archway – the hedge is some 4 metres high at this point – into the garden. This hedge was planted in 1927 by Angus Scott's grandfather and is kept in immaculate order today by Angus himself.

The homestead was built in the 1830s by one James Hill, a free settler who came out with Colonel Paterson in 1804 and was later given a grant of 1300 acres. His original home was destroyed by fire in 1864 and the present house was built then. It was not until 1878 that the property came into the hands of the Scott family, where it has remained until the present day.

The magnificent garden that surrounds the house today is in large part the work of Annabel Scott. She and Angus came to Dunedin in 1973 when she was a young bride. The old house had not been lived in for thirteen years. It was shabby and dilapidated, dark and dismal.

Annabel was a city girl. She grew up in Sandy Bay in Hobart, looking down at the harbour. She knew little of gardening or of grazing. Her mother had loved her garden but by the time Annabel reached her teens her mother was an invalid. Her father loved his vegetable garden. She remembers that he kept a cow – unusual even in those days in fashionable Sandy Bay. He planted a row of *Cupressus torulosa* that are still to be seen against the skyline today, but the flower garden meant little to him. Annabel mowed the lawns – reluctantly and without enthusiasm. The garden was on a steep hillside and she used an old hand mower. She pulled out a few weeds now and then and enjoyed the yellow evening primroses that were her mother's favourites. That was more or less the extent of her gardening.

When she arrived at Dunedin the 'garden' consisted of the hedge – which even then was magnificent – and between it and the house no fewer than twenty-eight *Cupressus macrocarpa*. Dark and sombre, they effectively excluded all light and sunshine from the house and made planting anything else in the garden a futile exercise.

Gradually over the next few years the house was restored – an unattractive upstairs balcony (not original, a later addition) was removed, the old black paint stripped off the woodwork, plumbing installed. Then Annabel turned her attention to the garden. She was in her twenties with, by this time, three little children under three and a half.

The removal of the macrocarpas was the first priority. But the stumps remained in the ground and Annabel gardened round them. This accounts for the unusual width of the borders: she planted on either side of the stumps. The result today (the stumps have long since rotted away) is quite wonderful. The regular addition of sheep manure and leaf mould has made the soil rich and pliable. A double-sided border presents far more problems for the gardener than one that is viewed from one side only. Annabel's borders are viewed in some cases from all four sides.

The old palms near the house were removed and, aided by her mother-in-law who was

The hellebore known as
'Boughton Beauty' was named
for the garden of the famous
alpine specialist Valerie Finnis.
Opposite above Looking
back through the arch, from the
garden of Dunedin, one sees
the mellow brick stables.
Opposite below One of the many
rare plants in Annabel's garden,
this bulbinella was grown from
seed imported from South Africa.

a keen gardener, Annabel began to think about planting. The removal of the old trees meant that now sunshine was flooding into the garden. First she needed a windbreak on the south side – the north was protected by the hedge. Influenced perhaps by her father, she planted thirty torulosas behind the orchard. They need no trimming and little attention.

Annabel's garden was never planned. It only developed, she says, when the children grew older, the sand pit and swings went and the cricket stopped on the front lawn. The old swamp cypress (*Taxodium distichum*) in the middle of the lawn survived it all and still dominates the garden today, although being planted on solid clay it has probably never reached its potential.

Early in her time at Dunedin Annabel fell in love with the rose. It was the first of a succession of passions. She joined the South Australian Rose Society, wrote to Ross Roses in Adelaide for a catalogue and sent in her first rose order. There are still many roses in the garden – perhaps a hundred, but they no longer hold pride of place. They fit into the mixed borders where they take what sun they can get and are unceremoniously removed if they fail to live up to expectations. The exception is the white Tea rose 'Mrs Herbert Stevens', which reaches to the eaves and greets the visitor on arrival.

Annabel's attention turned next to peonies, those wonderful and mysterious plants whose history Peter Valder tells us, in his splendid book *The Garden Plants of China*, goes well back into the first millennium BC. They delight in the cool-temperate climate of Tasmania. Annabel was captivated. She joined the American Paeony Society and started growing peonies from seed.

She became determined to learn more about plants. She did a course at the Launceston TAFE and worked for a time at a nursery in exchange for plants. It was while she was working with one of the nurserymen that the first double white hellebore turned up by chance in a Deloraine garden. This occasioned tremendous excitement and Annabel's thoughts turned to cross-pollinating and producing new strains. She grows hellebores now from seed procured from the Royal Horticultural Society in England and from the Alpine Garden Society. She has contacts all over the world. And Betty Ranicar, for whom the double white hellebore was named, gave her seeds of erythroniums that she had grown from seed brought with her from India. Today it grows almost like a weed in the garden at

Dunedin. The hellebores too – rich both in numbers and variety – are one of the glories of this remarkable garden. It was here that I first saw the variety called 'Boughton Beauty'. Once you start growing from seed, Annabel says, you are hooked. Annabel certainly was. She started growing perennials from seed.

Then the shade houses were built – five of them. They house about 500 pots – and not a sign of a weed in one of them. Some 200 pots are planted with seed. Every year Annabel resolves to cut back. And every year she plants more. Once the tiny seedlings emerge they are pricked out into individual pots and moved to a second shade house. Later they are moved into a third, where they stay until they are big enough to go into the garden.

Annabel is insatiable. She will go to any lengths to track down a new or especially fascinating variety. For a lover of plants this garden is tremendously exciting. No matter at what time of the year you visit it the garden will look superb and you will be certain of seeing things you have never come across before. The garden extends over something more than an acre – 2 acres if you include the orchard and tree plantation.

Gradually over the years as the trees Annabel planted near maturity the garden has changed from being a sunny, open one to what she has always dreamt of – a shady woodland garden. The emphasis is on the plants, not so much on design, although Annabel's innate sense of colour (she paints as well) ensures that the overall effect is harmonious.

Ornamentation is cut to a minimum. Annabel saved for months to buy the little bronze figure of Pan that stands among a group of flaxes and cordylines. Later she found Poppy – another bronze – to keep him company.

She corresponds with specialist nurseries, growers and enthusiasts in all corners of the globe. And visitors come in droves from all over Australia and from overseas. When asked about gardeners who have had the greatest influence on her she named the great English plantswoman Beth Chatto and the American writer Ken Druse, author of *The Collector's Garden*. She would probably say with him: 'I never met a plant I didn't like. Seeing a new one and then collecting it for my garden is my magnificent obsession.'

As is often the case in Tasmania, the garden at Dunedin surrounds a grand old house. The trees the Scotts have planted have had time to mature. The house is framed here by a fine pin oak on the left and a *Pyrus ussuriensis* on the right. The shrub borders are a mass of woodland plants.

The
species
roses

S OME EIGHT OR NINE years ago I was fortunate enough to meet the English
rosarian Hazel le Rougetel, who was in Australia on a lecture tour. She had
recently published a fascinating book entitled *A Heritage of Roses*. Her great
love was the old roses that at that time were not so often grown in private gardens. She toured the world in search of them and the book describes their cultivation in
the many countries she visited.

The following year we were in England and Hazel invited us to visit her. She was living at Liphook in Hampshire, an easy train ride from London. Her own garden was charming and contained more plants – both roses and others – than I thought could possibly
have been fitted into so small a space.

I had not realised what an important day this was to be for me. After lunch we were
taken to see several gardens Hazel was helping to design. The owner of one of them had
developed a passion for species roses. The garden was big – 5 or 6 acres – and the species
roses were growing not in beds, but in the grass as they would do in the wild. They were
neither pruned nor fertilised. There are no secateurs where they come from. Many of them
had grown into huge shrubs 3 to 5 metres high and just as wide. It was late summer so not
one of them was in flower. But the sight of *R. moyesii* 'Geranium' covered in its huge flagon-
shaped, scarlet hips is something I had never imagined in my wildest dreams. From that
moment I cherished an ambition to establish a collection of these intriguing plants.

We grew some of the species at Erinvale, but we didn't really have room for the sort of thing I envisaged. It was essentially a town garden surrounded by suburban homes. The species roses called for quite a different background. It was not until we came to Forest Hall that I had space enough and the right ambience for these wild roses.

Above all they need room. They cannot be crammed into garden beds and clipped and trimmed to make them adapt to the space available. They come from the wild and they must be permitted to grow as they grew in the mountains and by the streams of their native lands. Many of them, if unrestricted, reach giant proportions. Graham Thomas writes of a plant of *R. macrophylla* in the Cambridge Botanic Garden that reached approximately 6 metres in height and 8 metres in width. Forest Hall offers room enough even for this.

I'd made a start with species roses in the oak paddock. More could be planted between the parkland directly in front of the house and the daffodil paddock. They could take over the daffodil paddock entirely for that matter and the daffodils could come up around their feet. The roses would provide interest when the daffodils were over.

The species roses come from all parts of the northern hemisphere but none from the southern hemisphere. There are no roses native to Australia. Even the little dog rose that grows wild in the hedges of Tasmania and has become something of a pest to farmers has been introduced. Nevertheless they flourish here – perhaps because of the island's mild climate.

The species roses flower in spring or, in some cases, early summer and they do not repeat the performance in autumn. However, many of them have striking autumn foliage and even more of them have spectacular hips that follow their flowering. They are tough and hardy and once they are established they ask almost nothing of the gardener.

The first one I planted in the front garden was of course the one that had so impressed me on the day we spent with Hazel and which gave the impetus to this undertaking – *R. moyesii* 'Geranium'. I planted three together beside a huge boulder. In three years they towered above my head. The small flowers – about the size of a 50-cent piece – are red. It is a red like none other. A quite wonderful red. Not cherry red or crimson or scarlet, and with no trace of purple or orange. A stunning, clear, dark red, with golden stamens. They are borne in profusion in spring and are followed by those spectacular flagon-shaped hips – green at first, then turning to orange, then to scarlet. They hang on well into winter.

R. *moyesii* itself was discovered in China in 1890. Graham Thomas describes it as 'one of the finest of all flowering shrubs and one of E. A. Wilson's greatest treasures from the Far East'. It was named for the Reverend J. Moyes, a missionary who accompanied Wilson on his plant-hunting expeditions. It will grow to 4 metres. Having read Graham Thomas's description, I could not resist planting R. *moyesii* as well as its hybrids so put it beside the great boulder next to 'Geranium'. This hybrid was bred at Wisley in 1938 and is without doubt the favourite of the several hybrids that have been released. An earlier seedling is 'Highdownensis', which is almost as lovely. It has the same striking hips but the flowers are a pinkish cerise red. I planted five in the same vicinity and am anticipating impatiently the time when all nine of them come into flower or hip at once.

This was the beginning of a species collection.

The next lot to be planted were five plants of R. *willmottiae*. This was named for the famous English rosarian Ellen Willmott. She published between 1910 and 1914 the most beautiful rose book I have ever held in my hands. Called *The Genus Rosa*, it is illustrated with exquisite, full-page, botanically accurate paintings by Alfred Parsons. Many of the roses were growing in Miss Willmott's own extensive gardens at Great Warley. She was a woman of distinction – very beautiful, wickedly extravagant and decidedly eccentric. She was a scientist and a historian as well as being a great gardener and her enthusiasm extended far beyond roses. She was awarded the Medal of Honour in Horticulture. Her perhaps even more famous contemporary Gertrude Jekyll described her as 'the greatest of living woman gardeners'. High praise indeed.

My own plants of R. *willmottiae* have grown apace and are now over 3 metres high – and will probably exceed this. The beautiful ferny foliage is blue-green, the tiny flowers, not bigger than a 20-cent piece, are lilac pink and are followed by tiny, bright red hips. In the midst of a clump of three I planted the blue clematis 'Lady Betty Balfour', which is reputed not to mind full sun.

Opposite The flagon-shaped, scarlet hips of *R. moyesii* 'Geranium' follow the dramatic single red flowers and hang on well into winter.

Nearby I put three plants of *R. cinnamomea* (synonymous with *R. majalis*), which had its home in north-eastern Europe. The flowers are deep pink and are borne in clusters. A possum or a padimelon dug out one of the plants but the remaining two are doing well.

High up in the daffodil paddock is a collection of the early-flowering species *R. hugonis*, the Golden Rose of China, which is usually the first to flower – tiny, palest creamy yellow flowers on arching stems, with dark green ferny foliage and, later, dark red hips.

Next to it is *R. xanthina* 'Canary Bird', which grows wild in China, Mongolia and Turkestan. The foliage is similar to that of *R. hugonis* but the flowers are a brighter, sunnier yellow. It has quickly grown into a large shrub.

Then comes *R. ecae*, which flowers very early with the banksia roses. It came to England from Afghanistan in 1880 and the single blooms look surprisingly like buttercups.

Here too are several plants of *R. × alba* 'Semi-plena', which with its semi-single pure white blooms and the grey-green foliage typical of the albas must be one of the loveliest of all white roses.

Further down the slope is *R. eglanteria*, the Sweet Briar, remembered with affection by all who have driven down English country lanes or browsed in English cottage gardens – not so much for its tiny pink flowers or equally tiny red hips, but for the perfume exuded from its leaves, a perfume that suggests green apples. That great rosarian Dean Hole wrote that 'not even among the roses shall we find a more delicious perfume'. The Sweet Briar is remembered too by all lovers of Shakespeare's *A Midsummer-Night's Dream*, where it is described with the Musk roses on 'a bank where the wild thyme blows'.

The scent of the foliage so intrigued Lord Penzance, a noted English judge, that he decided to cross *R. eglanteria* with several Hybrid Perpetuals and Bourbons, hoping to raise new roses with aromatic foliage. In 1890 he released 'Lord Penzance' but in this rose *R. eglanteria* was crossed not with a Hybrid Perpetual or with a Bourbon but with the American rose known as 'Harison's Yellow' or the 'Yellow Rose of Texas'. It resembles the Sweet Briar in that it forms a dense shrub, with palest yellow flowers, and has the desired scented foliage. In 1894 Lord Penzance released 'Lady Penzance'. The other parent in this case was the dramatic *R. foetida* 'Bicolor'. 'Lady Penzance' was a great success. The little flowers are coppery pink and the foliage distinctly perfumed. I planted three each of the delightful little Penzance roses – closely together so that the branches are intertwined and the yellow and pink roses give the impression of growing on the same bush.

No planting of species roses would be complete without *R. foetida*, the Austrian Briar, and its relations. *R. foetida* came to Europe from Asia as early as the sixteenth century. The clear, bright yellow colouring was totally unknown among European roses. Later this rose was used extensively for breeding purposes and has been responsible for the emphatic yellow of many modern roses. The single, buttercup-yellow flowers are a delight and the stems are an intriguing mahogany colour. The shrub will grow to 2 metres or more. Unfortunately it and many of its relatives and descendants are particularly subject to black spot.

Anyone impressed by *R. foetida* will assuredly want to plant *R. foetida* 'Bicolor', which is similar in most respects but its flowers are striking and unusual in that the upper surface of the petals is a bright coppery scarlet while the underside is yellow. The third member of the group is *R. foetida* 'Persiana' (the Persian Yellow Rose), which differs from the other two in that the bright yellow flowers are very double. Like *R. foetida*, it has been extensively used in hybridising. Again I planted three each of these roses as a group.

My interest in the roses of Alister Clark made the inclusion of *R. gigantea*, which he used repeatedly in his breeding programme, essential. It is a fascinating rose. It is native to Burma and north-east India, and there will climb as high as 25 metres through branches of trees. Sir Henry Collett described having seen it through his field glasses at a distance of 3 kilometres. The great single, ivory-white flowers are so strongly perfumed that Roy Lancaster in his *Travels in China* said it enabled one to 'detect the presence of this rose in thick scrub long before it is located'.

I planted mine at the foot of a hoary chestnut on the drive. On the opposite side its hybrid, Alister Clark's 'Mrs Richard Turnbull', was planted beside a tall stump that I think had been another chestnut. 'Mrs Richard Turnbull' grew at an amazing pace – faster than any other rose in the garden – and is now at least 5 metres high. She would probably be more but she has exceeded her support. *R. gigantea* itself proved to be a special favourite with the possums, who chopped it down every time it put out a new shoot so that it has been left far behind. Why they liked one so much more than the other I have never discovered. The erection of the electric fence round the garden has resulted in a great improvement.

I have always loved Wolley Dod's Rose, R. *pomifera* 'Duplex'. The soft grey-green foliage is a perfect foil for the ingenuous fresh pink of the flowers. These are followed by attractive hips. I think I am prejudiced in favour of its breeder – one of those English country clergymen who made such an important contribution to English gardens (I think of Dean Hole, Canon Ellacombe, the Reverend Joseph Pemberton, the Reverend Foster Melliar, to mention only a few). Gertrude Jekyll in *A Gardener's Testament* described Wolley Dod as 'scholar, botanist and great English gentleman, an enthusiast for plant life, an experienced gardener and the kindest of instructors'. After reading her testimonial it would be impossible not to plant his rose.

In this area too I planted three of the Chestnut Rose, R. *roxburghii*. I had seen it first years ago in the garden of Olive Room in Launceston, where it had suckered and spread to such an extent that the whole bed had been taken over and the path rendered impassable. Roy Lancaster confirmed that this is its customary behaviour. It can apparently grow to 5 metres high and as much across so requires 'plenty of elbow room'. But he cherished nevertheless a great admiration for it. Describing a group of them, he wrote 'their crowning glory were the fruits, large yellowish prickle clad hips', which 'when mature fall to form a thick carpet on the ground and smell of apples ripening in a loft'. R. *roxburghii* was named for Dr William Roxburgh, who was for many years until 1813 in charge of the East India Company's Botanic Garden in Calcutta.

Closer to the house I planted a group of the entrancing Damask rose 'Ispahan' (or 'Rose d'Isfahan'), which grows wild on the hills of Iran. It came to England early in the nineteenth century from the Middle East. It is not a species rose but appreciates the space and freedom accorded to them. The double pink blooms are deliciously fragrant and borne over an exceptionally long period.

———

Opposite Perhaps the most arresting sight in the garden in autumn is
R. *sweginzowii*, with its deep blue-green foliage, its mahogany-coloured
stems, its huge thorns (not visible on this young branch) and its clusters
of scarlet hips.

I have included a group of American roses: *R. californica* 'Plena', with delightful pink blooms borne on arching canes; *R. virginiana*, remarkable for its intense autumn colour; *R. woodsii*, with its lilac-pink flowers, colourful hips and a vigorous suckering habit; and *R. setigera*, the Prairie Rose, which puts forth long, lax, procumbent canes and also suckers freely.

The list goes on. The one that gives me the greatest joy so far goes by the impossible name of *R. sweginzowii*. It comes from China as so many superb plants do. It is not grown primarily for its flowers – they are small, no bigger than a 50-cent piece, and of a bright Barbara Cartland pink. But the foliage is an entrancing blue-green, the stems a rich mahogany brown. The thorns, huge and a translucent red, almost rival those of *R. omeiensis pteracantha* (synonymous with *R. sericea pteracantha*, the Wing Thorn Rose). The hips are brilliant scarlet and flagon-shaped, like those of *R. moyesii* 'Geranium', and they hang in great clusters. In fact this rose has everything. In autumn it is without doubt the chief attraction of the garden. I was so fascinated with my first group of three that I have planted another group on the far side of the daffodil paddock.

By now the sunny corners in the oak paddock were all taken up and I didn't really want any more species roses in the front garden. When I came across three fine plants of 'Kazanlik' (*R. damascena* 'Trigintipetala'), I was at a loss where to plant them. This is the rose, so Graham Thomas tells us, used 'more than any other in Bulgaria for the production of "attar"'. A place had to be found for it.

I contemplated planting it on the shores of the lake. However, this would probably not meet with Bill's approval. The lake paddock has become his province. Fishing stops in Tasmania after Easter, when snow falls on the mountains and the roads become icy. From then until late spring Bill does not go up to the Great Lake. The boat comes down for servicing, fishing gear is checked and mended and put away, and a seemingly endless succession of fishless days stretches ahead.

This could scarcely be borne by Bill when he retired to Forest Hall. One sunny day in late April we drove to Bridport on the north coast and came home with no fewer than 300 commercially bred yearling trout. These were put into our lake, and several times a week Bill sets out at dusk with the dogs and they walk round the lake scattering largesse in the form of fish pellets. In a year or two these trout will be big enough to catch.

Bill has taken over the responsibility too of watering the five scarlet oaks on the far bank. The little plantation of Yunnan poplars also initially had a tenuous hold on life. It was Bill who cherished and watered them.

Wanting more brilliant autumn colour, we planted near the oaks a golden ash, a claret ash and *Acer negundo* 'Sensation'. At the furthest point we put three dark green pencil pines. All of these had to be watered for the first year or so, and in the absence of taps they had to be watered by bucket. This Bill did. These trees, rather than the roses, are his love. It would not be fair or reasonable to start planting roses here.

A couple of months ago we acquired a small wooden dinghy, which we moor at the edge of the lake. On tranquil evenings when the fishing season is officially over, Bill takes his line and rows out into the middle of the lake accompanied invariably by Willy's successor, an ebullient red heeler named Tom.

'Kazanlik' will have to be planted somewhere in the daffodil paddock.

With the advent of the trout, Bill took full charge of the lake,
watering and caring for the young trees to ensure that it becomes
a thing of beauty.

Epilogue

THE GARDEN AT Forest Hall is young. But roses establish quickly and in four or five years we should begin to see the results of our labours. The fences should be hidden behind walls of rambling roses. Young trees will begin to make their presence felt. Climbing roses will reach to the top of their supports and send down showers of blossom. Bulbs will form thicker and thicker carpets.

But I share the sentiments of the Australian poet Rosemary Dobson: 'The poem you see in your mind is always better than the reality you set down on paper. You never reach it 100%. There is always something which eludes one . . . a search for something only fugitively glimpsed.' Her words could as well have been written by a gardener as a poet. For the garden is never finished, gardeners are never finally satisfied with their creation.

Gardening is a complex activity that can be undertaken on many levels. But always, whether one is growing petunias in a pot or designing a landscape, one is looking forward, striving to see a vision materialise. Gardeners are essentially positive people.

To be a full-time gardener in one's own garden is one of the richest and most rewarding of occupations. But it must not be entered upon lightly. Only if it is a firm commitment can it provide real satisfaction. And first one has to cast aside the prevailing ethic that regards activity undertaken for financial gain as the only kind to be taken seriously. The rewards from the garden are rich beyond all measure – but none of them are monetary.

The gardens of the old monasteries served a very practical purpose. They fed and nourished whole communities. But they also served a symbolic purpose. And they inspired prayer and meditation. So it is with gardens – even in this materialistic age. Serious gardeners regard their gardens as something more than a pastime, something undertaken to amuse themselves. Even if they never verbalise it, they probably see the role of the gardener much as Rosemary Dobson sees the role of the poet – as 'keeping alive the things of the mind and things of the spirit'.

Roses at Forest Hall

'Abraham Darby'
'Adélaide d'Orléans'
× *alba* 'Maxima'
× *alba* 'Semi-plena'
'Albéric Barbier'
'Albertine'
'Alister Stella Gray'
'Altissimo'
'Amadis'
'Angel Face'
'Anna Maria de
    Montravel'
'Archduke Charles'
'Arethusa'
'Assemblage des
    Beautés'
'Australia Felix'
'Autumnalis'
'Awakening'

'Ballerina'
'Barney Hutton'
    (not registered)
'Baronne Henriette de
    Snoy'
'Beauty of Glenhurst'
'Beauty of Rosemawr'
'Belle de Crécy'
'Belle Story'
'Betsy Taaffe'
'Blaze Superior'
'Bleak House'
'Bloomfield Abundance'
'Bloomfield Courage'
'Bloomfield Dainty'
'Bonica'
'Bourbon Queen'
'Buff Beauty'

'Camellia Rose'
'Canary Bird'
'Canterbury'
'Carabella'
'Cardinal de Richelieu'
'Céline Forestier'

'Cerise Bouquet'
'Charles de Mills'
'Château de Clos
    Vougeot'
'Cherub'
'Chianti'
'China Doll'
'Cicely Lascelles'
'Cicely O'Rorke'
'Claire Jacquier'
'Cloth of Gold'
'Commandant
    Beaurepaire'
'Complicata'
'Comtesse du Cayla'
'Constance Spry'
'Cornelia'
'Corylus'
'Courier'
'Cracker'
'Cramoisi Supérieur'
'Crépuscule'
'Cupid'
'Cymbeline'

'Dainty Bess'
'Dapple Dawn'
'Daydream'
'Delicata'
'Devon'
'Devoniensis'
'Dorothy Perkins'
'Duchess of Portland'
'Duchesse de Brabant'
'Duchesse de
    Montebello'
'Dunwich Rose'
'Dupontii'

'Editor Stewart'
'Edna Walling Rose'
    (not registered)
'Elina'
'Elmshorn'
'English Elegance'

'Erfurt'

'F. J. Grootendorst'
'Fantin Latour'
'Felicia'
'Félicité et Perpétue'
'Fellemberg'
'Fisherman's Friend'
'Fortune's Double
    Yellow'
'Francesca'
'Francis E. Lester'
'Frau Karl Druschki'
'Fritz Nobis'
'Fru Dagmar Hastrup'
'Frühlingsduft'
'Frühlingsgold'
'Frühlingsmorgen'

'Général Galliéni'
'Général Jacqueminot'
'Général Schablikine'
'Geranium'
'Gloire de Dijon'
'Gloire de Guilan'
'Glory of Edzell'
'Gold Bunny'
'Golden Celebration'
'Golden Vision'
'Golden Wings'
'Goldfinch'
'Graham Thomas'
'Great Maiden's
    Blush'
'Gruss an Aachen'
'Gwen Nash'

'Heidekönigin'
'Heidesommer'
'Heritage'
'Hermosa'
'Hero'
'Hiawatha'
'Highdownensis'
'Honorine de Brabant'

'Howard Florey'
'Hume's Blush
    Tea-scented China'

'Iced Ginger'
'Immortal Juno'
'Irish Rich Marbled'
'Ispahan'

'Jacques Cartier'
'James Mitchell'
'Jaquenetta'
'Jayne Austin'
'Jean Ducher'
'Jean Galbraith'
'Jeanne Lajoie'
'Jessie Clark'
'John Clare'
'John S. Armstrong'
'Julia's Rose'
'Just Joey'

'Kathleen Harrop'
'Katie Pianto's Rose'
    (not registered)
'Kazanlik'
'Kent'
'Kitty Kininmonth'

'L. D. Braithwaite'
'La France'
'Lady Hillingdon'
'Lady Medallist'
'Lady Penzance'
'Lamarque'
'Laura Davoust'
'Laura Louisa'
'Lavender Lassie'
'Lavender Pinocchio'
'Lawrence Johnston'
'Le Vésuve'
'Leda'
'Leverkusen'
'Light Touch'
'Lord Penzance'

'Lorraine Lee'
'L'Ouche'
'Louis XIV'
'Lucetta'

'Maigold'
'Manettii'
'Marie van Houtte'
'Martha'
'May Queen'
'Mermaid'
'Midnight Sun'
'Milkmaid'
'Mme Alfred Carrière'
'Mme Alice Garnier'
'Mme Caroline Testout'
'Mme de Tartas'
'Mme Driout'
'Mme Ernst Calvat'
'Mme Grégoire
    Staechelin'
'Mme Isaac Pereire'
'Monsieur Tillier'
'Moonbeam'
'Moonsprite'
'Morletii'
'Moth'
'Mrs Fred Danks'
'Mrs John Laing'
'Mrs Mary Thomson'
'Mrs Oakley Fisher'
'Mrs Oswin's Gigantea'
    (not registered)
'Mrs Richard Turnbull'
'Mutabilis'

'Nancy Hayward'
'Narrow Water'
'New Dawn'
'Niree Hunter'
    (not registered)
'Noble Anthony'

'Octavius Weld'
    (not registered)
'Old Blush'
'Othello'

'Parks' Yellow Tea-
    scented China'
'Paul Ricault'

'Pax'
'Peach Blossom'
'Penelope'
'Penelope' (Tea)
'Perle d'Or'
'Philanderer'
    (not registered)
'Phyllis Bide'
'Pierre de Ronsard'
'Pinkie'
'Princess of Wales'

'Quatre Saisons'

'Rambling Rector'
'Ravensworth'
'Red Coat'
'Red Meidiland'
'Redouté'
'Regensberg'
'Reine des Violettes'
'Renae'
'Restless'
'Ringlet'
'Rosa Mundi' (R. gallica
    'Versicolor')
'Rose Romantic'
'Rose-Marie Viaud'
'Roseraie de l'Haÿ'
'Rosy Cushion'
'Rugspin'

'Safrano'
'Sally Holmes'
'Sarah van Fleet'
'Scabrosa'
'Scarlet Queen
    Elizabeth'
'Scepter'd Isle'
'Schneezwerg'
'Sea Foam'
'Seduction'
'Semperflorens'
'Sheila Bellair'
'Shropshire Lass'
'Single Cherry'
'Slater's Crimson China'
'Soleil d'Or'
'Sombreuil'
'Sophy's Rose'
'Souvenir d'Alphonse

    Lavallée'
'Souvenir de la
    Malmaison'
'Souvenir de Mme
    Léonie Viennot'
'Souvenir de St
    Anne's'
'Sparrieshoop'
'Spring Song'
'Squatter's Dream'
'Stanwell Perpetual'
'Stephanie's Gallica'
    (not registered)
'Stephen Porter'
    (not registered)
'Suitor'
'Sunny South'
'Surrey'
'Sussex'
'Sutter's Gold'
'Sympathie'

'Tess of the
    d'Urbervilles'
'The Bishop'
'The Pilgrim'
'Tipsy Imperial
    Concubine'
'Tonner's Fancy'
'Tour de Malakoff'
'Tradescant'
'Triomphe de
    Luxembourg'
'Troilus'
'Tuscany Superb'
'Twilight Glow'

'Vanity'
'Veilchenblau'
'Violette'
'Viridiflora'

'White Meidiland'
'White Wings'
'Wildflower'
'William Lobb'
'William Shakespeare'
'William III'
'Windrush'

'Zéphirine Drouhin'

SPECIES ROSES

R. acicularis
R. anemonoides
R. beggeriana
R. blanda
R. bracteata
R. brunonii
R. californica 'Plena'
R. centifolia 'Parvifolia'
R. cinnamomea
R. ecae
R. eglanteria
R. farreri 'Persetosa'
R. fedtschenkoana
R. foetida
R. foetida 'Bicolor'
R. foetida 'Persiana'
R. forrestiana
R. glauca
R. gigantea
R. gymnocarpa
R. hemisphaerica
R. holodonta
R. hugonis
R. macrophylla
R. × micrugosa
R. moyesii
R. multiflora 'Grevillei'
    (syn. R. multiflora
    'Platyphylla')
R. nutkana
R. omeiensis pteracantha
    (syn. R. sericea
    pteracantha)
R. pendulina
R. pomifera 'Duplex'
R. primula
R. roxburghii
R. rugosa 'Alba'
R. setigera
R. spinosissima
    'Altaica'(syn.
    R. pimpinellifolia
    'Grandiflora')
R. spinosissima
    'Lutea Maxima'
R. sweginzowii
R. virginiana
R. willmottiae
R. woodsii

Acknowledgements

I would like to thank the owners of the gardens featured in this book. Such gardens are only created as a result of true dedication, knowledge and very hard work. I extend my warm thanks to Judy Humphreys; Michael McWilliams; John and Sophie Ranicar; Annabel Scott; and also to Piers Ranicar for lending me his mother's priceless garden diaries.

I would like to thank Tim Barbour not only for coming on a wild, windy, wet day to draw the map of the garden – and subsequently putting up cheerfully with our many changes – but also for allowing us to photograph his own garden.

In questions of spelling, classification and nomenclature I have been guided by Graham Thomas. It was his books I turned to when I first started to grow roses, and he is still a constant source of inspiration and information.

The extract on page 88 from Ethel Turner's *The Ungardeners*, originally published by Ward Lock & Co. in 1925, is reproduced with the kind permission of her grand-daughter Philippa Poole.

Many people are involved in the production of a book such as this. I am grateful to the expert team at Penguin Books, who are always a delight to work with. I would especially like to thank Executive Publisher Julie Gibbs; Lesley Dunt, the editor of the book, with whom I have spent many (often hilarious) hours on the phone; Jane Drury and Kirsten Abbott for additional editorial help; Senior Production Controller Carmen de la Rue; and Tony Palmer, for his artistic handling of the design.

Above all, I am profoundly grateful to Simon Griffiths for his outstanding photography and for his willingness to fly down to Tasmania to catch things just at the right moment.

Index

Rose cultivars are listed by individual name; species and their near hybrids under *Rosa*.
Page numbers in *italic* refer to photograph captions.

INDEX

'Great Maiden's Blush'
261
'Gruss an Aachen' 163,
261
Gubbins, Bridget 113
Gunnera manicata 75, 76
Gurr, Matthew 233
'Gwen Nash' 261

'Harison's Yellow' 252
Harkness, Jack 55, 130,
200
hawthorns 10, 26, 73, 222
red 33, *210*, 213
tansy-leaved 109
'Heidekönigin' 261
'Heidesommer' 261
Helichrysum italicum subsp.
serotinum 180
hellebores *see Helleborus*
Helleborus 95, 96
'Betty Ranicar' 98, *98*,
225, 244
corsicus 224
orientalis 224
× *sternii* 'Boughton
Beauty' 224, *242*,
245
Hemerocallis fulva 'Flore
Pleno' 232
'herb garden' *152*, 154–5,
157
'Heritage' 85, *85*, 261
'Hermosa' 200, 261
'Hero' 261
'Hiawatha' 261
Hidcote Manor 55
'Highdownensis' 251, 261
Himalayan Musk Rose 158
Hole, Dean Reynolds 85,
252, 255
hollies 11, 128, 192, 204,
206
Great-aunt Mary's 93,
95, 125
variegated 93
honesty 93
'Honorine de Brabant'
108, *110*, *115*, 261
'Howard Florey' 45, 261
'Hume's Blush Tea-scented
China' 197, 200, 261
Humphreys, Judy 142,
144–5
Huxley, Ian 80
Hydrangea
quercifolia 148
'Snow Cap' 148

'Iced Ginger' 261

'Immortal Juno' 82, 84,
85, 261
Iris *146*, 217, *219*, 220–1
cristata 221
innominata 108, 221
japonica 221
kaempferi (water iris)
27, 29, 75, 76, 220–1
ochroleuca (swamp iris)
27, 217, 220
'Professor Blaauw' 69
pseudacorus (water flag)
27, 70, 76, 217, 222
reticulata 'Harmony'
221
sibirica 27, 220–1
unguicularis 217
× *xiphium* 88, 217
'Irish Rich Marbled' 149,
152, 155, 261
'Ispahan' 255, 261

Jacobite Rose 108
'Jacques Cartier' 178, 261
'James Mitchell' 261
Japanese snowbell 109
Japanese windflower 93
japonicas 92
'Jaquenetta' 44, 261
Jasminum polyanthum 52,
188
'Jayne Austin' 261
'Jean Ducher' 43, 261
'Jean Galbraith' *64*, 67,
68, 69, 261
'Jeanne Lajoie' 261
Jekyll, Gertrude 62, 220,
251, 255
'Jessie Clark' 77, 80, 261
'Joanna Hill' 54
'John Clare' 66, 261
'John S. Armstrong' 178,
261
Johnson, Hugh 73
Johnston, Lawrence 55
Jolly Farmer 70, 72–6, 75
jonquils 31, 33, 45
Joyce, Ray 113, 232
'Jude the Obscure' 66
'Julia Clements' 48
'Julia's Rose' 47, *47*, 48–9,
50, 261
'Just Joey' 45, 261

'Kathleen Harrop' 233,
235, 261
'Katie Pianto's Rose' 261
'Kazanlik' 256, 257, 261
'Kent' 201, *203*, 261
Kerria japonica 52

Kingsley, Rose 40
kitchen garden 77–88
'Kitty Kininmonth' 261
kniphofia 237
Knorr, Hans 96, 121, 124
Kordes roses 54, 130,
132, 162

'L. D. Braithwaite' 176,
261
'La France' 261
lachenalias *146*
ladies' eardrops 201
'Lady Hillingdon' 44–5,
145, 261
'Lady Medallist' 213, 261
'Lady Penzance' 252–3,
261
'Lady Seton' 48
lake 23, *24*, 26–7, 29, 30,
256, 258
'Lamarque' 113, 261
larch 10, 189, 192, 232–3
'Laura Davoust' 261
'Laura Louisa' 261
laurel 34, 45
Lavandula
dentata 141, 179
stoechas *210*, 212
'Lavender Lassie' 162,
261
'Lavender Pinocchio' 47,
163, 261
'Lawrence Johnston' 55,
56, 261
Law-Smith, Joan 52,
67–8, 95
le Rougetel, Hazel 248
'Le Vésuve' 163, 200–1,
261
'Leda' 261
Levens Hall 184, 185
'Leverkusen' 54, *60*, 261
'Light Touch' 261
lilac 41, 92
lime tree, weeping silver
192
lindens 11, *174*, 192
Liriodendron tulipifera
193
Lonicera nitida 90, 93
'Lord Penzance' 252, 261
'Lorraine Lee' 144, 262
'L'Ouche' 201, 262
'Louis XIV' 201, 262
'Lucetta' 262
Lunaria annua 93

MacCrae, Mary 19
macleaya 172

McMurtrie, Mary 155,
157
McWilliams, Michael 72,
73, 75, 76
Magnolia
'Caerhayes Belle' 148
grandiflora 89, 109
'Heaven Scent' 148
'Star Wars' 108, 148
Magnolia Rose 128
'Maigold' 54, 62, 262
Malus
aldenhamensis 185
floribunda (Japanese crab
apple) 108, 139
'Golden Hornet'
108–9, 139
hillieri 140
ioensis 139
'Jack Humm' 140
'John Downie' 139,
139
toringoides 108
trilobata 140
'Manettii' 262
'Maréchal Niel' 58
'Marie van Houtte' 44,
262
'Martha' 262
'Mary Rose' 113
'May Queen' 262
medlar trees 109
Melliar, Rev. Foster 255
'Mermaid' 232, 262
Mertensia asiatica 172
'Midnight Sun' 85, 262
Miles, Todd 235
'Milkmaid' 262
'Mme Abel Chatenay'
144, 209
'Mme Alfred Carrière' 262
'Mme Alice Garnier'
128–9, 213, 216, 262
'Mme Caroline Testout'
81, 262
'Mme de Tartas' 81, *165*,
262
'Mme Driout' 130, 262
'Mme Ernst Calvat' 84,
262
'Mme Grégoire Staechelin'
126, 128, 262
'Mme Hardy' 68
'Mme Isaac Pereire' 262
'Mme Pierre Oger' 68
mock orange 89
'Monsieur Tillier' 262
montbretias 95
'Moonbeam' 262
'Moonsprite' 59, 262

266

THE GARDEN AT FOREST HALL

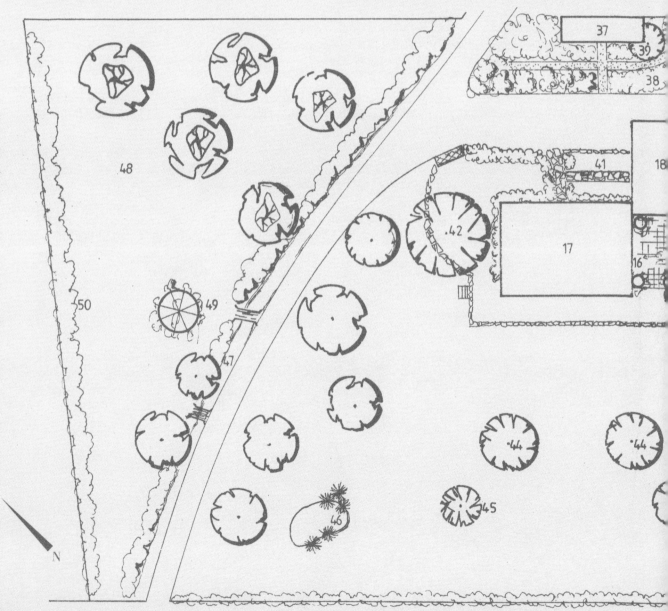